What People Are Saying About *Spiritual Breakthrough...*

Sue Curran has done it again with a book that addresses two subjects: true freedom and full healing. I recommend this valuable book to all who desire to face the challenges of physical and emotional sicknesses and generate the faith to experience true breakthrough.

—*Dr. Myles Munroe*
President and founder, Bahamas Faith Ministries International
Nassau, Bahamas

Sue Curran's insightful book *Spiritual Breakthrough* will show you how to move from just surviving to *really living*; how to obtain the life you've always wanted. Curran's ministry has brought help and healing to thousands of people around the world. This work will give you the practical tools you need to break bondages, so that you may receive healing from the emotional pain, loss, and trauma that hold you back from experiencing God's best. If you've been searching for a way to let go of the past and make the most of your future, this book is for you!

—*Cheryl Sacks*
Author, *The Prayer-Saturated Church*; coauthor, *Prayer-Saturated Kids*;
Cofounder, BridgeBuilders International Leadership Network
Phoenix, Arizona

D1450885

Spiritual BREAK THROUGH

SUE CURRAN

WHITAKER
HOUSE

SPIRITUAL BREAKTHROUGH:
Healing and Wholeness for the Soul

Sue Curran
www.suecurran.com

ISBN: 978-1-60374-959-6
eBook ISBN: 978-1-60374-983-1
Printed in the United States of America
© 2014 by Sue Curran

Whitaker House
1030 Hunt Valley Circle
New Kensington, PA 15068
www.whitakerhouse.com

Library of Congress Cataloging-in-Publication Data (Pending)

1 2 3 4 5 6 7 8 9 10 11 **W** 21 20 19 18 17 16 15 14

CONTENTS

HOW FREE IS FREE?

I once heard Oral Roberts say, "Miracles are wonderful—especially when you need one." Today, there is a growing awareness in believers of their paramount need for divine miracles in their personal lives. I am hearing the desperate cry of Christians who suffer from the oppression of mental and emotional hang-ups. They confide to me their bondages to all kinds of fears and tormenting confusion.

Some of these sincere believers sense that this deep spiritual need is keeping them from fulfilling God's destiny for their lives. They have read Jesus' promises of abundant life and divine peace and joy, which He died to give His followers. And they consider the promises of peace He gave to His disciples:

> *The thief cometh not, but for to steal, and to kill, and to destroy: I am come that they might have life, and that they might have it more **abundantly**.* (John 10:10)

> *Peace I leave with you, my peace I give unto you: not as the world giveth.... Let not your heart be troubled, neither let it be afraid.* (John 14:27)

Many Christians have listened to sermons and tried to walk in the biblical truth they have heard. If their sincerity or faithfulness could have done the work in them, they would have already been experiencing the freedom that Jesus promised them. Yet they find themselves unable to break out of their oppressive mental and emotional bondage.

Trying to cope daily with fear, anger, depression, and strained relationships, some followers have despaired that they will ever be any different. They wonder if the promises of God for abundant life are really true. Is it a false expectation, merely a fond dream? Or will Jesus really do what seems too good to be true? Will He open the door of their painful prisons and set them free?

One of the Greek words for *abundant* in the New Testament is *perisseuo*, which means "superfluous" or to have "enough and [some] to spare."[1] The good news of the gospel is that Jesus does not save you simply to take you to heaven when you die. He did not intend to leave you here on earth to live a life of physical, mental, and emotional pain. *Abundant living* in the peace and joy of Christ is to be the norm for all Christians. When you receive divine revelation of this truth, you will understand that the promises of Jesus are not too good to be true.

Freedom from mental and emotional bondage is part of the abundant life Jesus promised for you in every area of your Christian life. When you accepted Christ as your Savior, He gave to you the unfathomable gift of *sozo*[2]—His complete salvation that restores you to wholeness in your spirit, soul, and body.

> ### *Jesus does not save us simply to take us to heaven when we die.*

Jesus' approach to each pain-racked, pitiable person He encountered was to set them free from whatever bondage they suffered. From demoniacs to Pharisees—no one was exempt from His promise of abundant life, if they received the miraculous power of His love. He demonstrated His desire to transform their lives and declared that this was His purpose for coming to earth.

1. *Strong's*, #G4053.
2. *Strong's*, #G4982.

The Spirit of the Lord is upon me, because he hath anointed me to preach the gospel to the poor; he hath sent me to heal the brokenhearted, to preach deliverance to the captives, and recovering of sight to the blind, to set at liberty them that are bruised, to preach the acceptable year of the Lord. (Luke 4:18–19)

These painful conditions that Jesus read from Isaiah's scroll (see Isaiah 61) relate to the profound human need for wholeness, physically, mentally, and emotionally, which takes place in the soul. Jesus was anointed by the Father to preach the good news of healing to the brokenhearted, and deliverance to the captives, and to heal the blind and bruised. On Calvary, Jesus bought this freedom for every soul born into sin. He bore the stripes for our physical healing, and He carried our grief and sorrows with Him to the grave. (See Isaiah 53.)

Was He successful in His mission? Yes! He declared this fact one day in the synagogue: *"This day is this scripture fulfilled in your ears"* (Luke 4:21). And as He hung on the cross to save the world, He declared, *"It is finished"* (John 19:30)!

As believers on this earth, our lives should be characterized by the abundant life He died to give us. We should be enjoying freedom from the emotional and mental bondages of sin that cripple our souls—even after we are born again.

Contending For Sozo—the Abundant Life

Salvation, translated from the Greek word *sozo*[3] means to "deliver or protect," to "heal," "preserve," to "(make) whole." It is a picture of the abundant life Jesus promised. Too often, sincere believers settle for something much less than the wonderful freedom of *sozo*—complete salvation.

Many Christians love God and try to serve Him with their whole heart. But they continue to struggle with painful bondages, wondering what they are doing wrong. They have not understood the amazing provisions of Christ's salvation to make them whole, to deliver them from mental and emotional pain.

3. *Strong's*, #G4982.

How many people have had their destinies hijacked by Satan's lie: "You will always be like this; you will never change"? This is one of the reasons there are so many discouraged people in our churches. It just doesn't seem to work for them. And the enemy whispers, "Other people can enjoy freedom; but you're different. It won't work for you." But *sozo* means to deliver or to protect, to heal, to preserve, to make whole.

The Responsibility of All Believers

During more than four decades of pastoring, I have observed this deep need for deliverance and freedom many times in the lives of sincere believers. And I have sought God earnestly on how to minister His grace to them in the depth of their need. More recently, when I needed a miracle of healing in my own body, the Holy Spirit began to give me greater revelation of my personal need for wholeness in my soul. For many months, I sought God for my healing miracle, and I gained a deeper understanding of *"sozo* salvation" through Jesus' promise, *"If the Son therefore shall make you free, ye shall be free indeed"* (John 8:36).

As believers, we need to teach others to contend for the abundant life Jesus has promised. Otherwise, they will be unable to fulfill God's destiny for their lives. Often, we try to address symptoms of their emotional bondage, such as fear, anger, insecurity, loneliness—and the list goes on. We encourage people to try harder, to do better, failing to recognize the underlying problem. In doing so, we have helped them get rid of the bad *fruit* without dealing with the *root*.

Jeremiah blames the religious leaders of his day for superficially healing the people: *"They have healed also the hurt of the daughter of my people **slightly** ["superficially"* (NASB)] *saying, Peace, peace; when there is no peace"* (Jeremiah 6:14). These leaders ministered to the people superficially, even insincerely it seems, declaring peace to them when there was none. Unfortunately, as ministers of the gospel, we may be able to relate to these spiritual leaders that Jeremiah condemns.

My burning desire for the people under my care is to see them profoundly and completely healed—made whole—in their salvation experience. Jesus draws hurting people to His church to be made whole, not just slightly encouraged or temporarily comforted. My responsibility as a Christian leader is to contend for the wholeness that Jesus has promised. And, as I discover greater dimensions of walking in His truth, I must teach other believers to do the same.

> *Salvation does a complete work to set us free to live His abundant life.*

In 2010, during a ministry trip to Africa, I developed a very painful and debilitating illness. (See chapter 2 for full story.) The following months of intense suffering caused me to seek God for His healing and deliverance power in my life. As I did, the Holy Spirit shed new light on His desire and provision for me, as well as all believers, to walk in wholeness.

With new interest, I read the question Jesus asked the man lying at the pool of Bethesda: *"Wilt thou be made whole?"* (John 5:6). His question became for me a deeper revelation of the way Jesus healed. I began to understand that His way of healing was not to rebuke the man's laziness or lack of personal motivation; rather, He challenged him to pursue His promise. He was promising divine wholeness to this man, the one who had spent most of his life lying there in helplessness.

Wholeness Supersedes Healing

The Greek word for wholeness is *hugies*,[4] which means to be "healthy, sound, whole." Jesus did not simply ask the man at the pool of Bethesda if he wanted his lameness healed; He asked him if he wanted to be made *"whole."* Wholeness does not just relate to having a sound physical body; it includes divine health for your soul, which involves your mind, emotions, and will. Jesus came to create wholeness, from the inside out, and the wholeness that Jesus promised supersedes mere physical healing.

In ministering to people, I have observed that it is possible for believers to receive physical healing through prayer and the laying on of hands. But without being made whole in their minds, they may still be vulnerable to physical illness. Even medical research concurs with this phenomena—the mind contributes to many physical illnesses.

---

4. *Strong's*, #G5199.

Spirit

According to the Scriptures, mankind was created as a triune being; that is, man is made up of a spirit, a soul, and a body. Therefore, it is important to understand the work of salvation in your life when you are born again. When you receive Christ as your Savior, your spirit is born again in an instant. Your sins are forgiven, you receive eternal life, and you are placed into right relationship with God: "*Therefore being justified by faith, we have peace with God through our Lord Jesus Christ*" (Romans 5:1).

Soul

Still, the New Testament Scriptures clearly teach that there is an ongoing work of salvation, which is sometimes referred to as *sanctification*. This takes place in your soul, which is composed of the mind, the will, and the emotions. The apostle Paul taught on different facets of sanctification, using phrases like "*put off the old man*" (Colossians 3:9) and "*put on the new man*" (verse 10) to describe this work of the Holy Spirit to make believers whole in Christ. (See also Ephesians 4:22–24.)

The Mind. Furthermore, the apostle Paul taught that your mind must be *renewed* (see Romans 12:2), because the carnal mind is God's enemy. It is incapable of being subject to the law of God. (See Romans 8:6–8.) That means that without the Holy Spirit's work of transforming your thinking, you will be unable to understand the will of God. The Holy Spirit alone will lead you into all truth through His Word. He will teach you to think and reason in a way that is different from the learned patterns your carnal mind has dictated in the past.

The Will. The will is a gift from God that allows mankind to walk in relationship with its Creator. God's great heart of love could not be satisfied with "puppets" who submitted to Him because they had no recourse. Our Father wanted sons and daughters, created in His image, who would say yes to Him out of love, not obligation.

Because of this, God's "family" would forever be a testimony against Lucifer's great rebellion against His love in heaven.

Jesus came as the loving Son of God to show us that His will was submitted completely to the Father's will. He modeled for us the correct response to the Father's love, declaring that He did nothing except what the Father had first shown Him:

> I am able to do nothing from Myself [independently, of My own accord— but only as I am taught by God and as I get His orders]....I do not seek or consult My own will [I have no desire to do what is pleasing to Myself, My own aim, My own purpose] but only the will and pleasure of the Father Who sent Me.   (John 5:30 AMP)

Because of the fall of mankind in original sin, you were born with a sinful nature that is against God and does not submit to His love. And before you are born again, you walk in your carnal nature, making independent choices to rule your own life. But when you surrender your life to Christ, you begin to learn how to surrender your life decisions, both big and small, to God. As you continue to do so, you will learn to walk in the freedom of Christ, and the Holy Spirit will empower you to fulfill His destiny for your life.

The Emotions. In every life situation, Jesus' emotional responses were fueled by the love of God. Likewise, your emotions must be continually transformed so that they express the love of God in all of life's situations. The Scriptures clearly teach clearly that your *sozo*, or wholeness, involves replacing negative emotions like anger, hatred, and jealousy with the fruit of the Spirit: "*love, joy, peace, longsuffering, kindness, goodness,* [and] *faith*" (Galatians 5:22).

Yet Christians who have walked with God for many years are still slaves to their negative emotional responses. As a result, they continually cause grief and pain to themselves and others. Without experiencing *sozo* wholeness, they cannot enjoy the peace and joy that Jesus promised His kingdom followers. They have yet to experience the reality that Jesus, as the Author and Finisher of their faith (see Hebrews 12:2), has promised to present us faultless before His throne:

> And the very God of peace sanctify you wholly; and I pray God your whole spirit and soul and body be preserved blameless unto the coming of our Lord Jesus Christ. Faithful is he that calleth you, who also will do it.
>   (1 Thessalonians 5:23–24)

Healed and Made Whole

The Lord showed me that wholeness is possible only when those crooked, carnal bondages in our soul have been dealt with and healed. This ongoing work of *sozo* will result in the outward manifestation of health in our bodies, as well. As I mentioned, medical doctors and psychologists are acknowledging that mental and emotional turmoil can actually cause some diseases.

The good news is that our Creator-Redeemer understood the complexities of His creation and the dreadful plight of fallen man. When the blood of Christ is applied to our lives continually, we can receive wholeness and live the abundant life He died to give to every believer.

A Second Touch

I believe there is a revelation of truth for us in seeing not only *what* Jesus does but *how* He does it. Have you ever wondered why Jesus approached healing in a variety of ways? For example, when He went to Bethsaida, some people brought a blind man to Him, asking for His touch. Instead, Jesus took the man by the hand and led him outside of town, *"and when [Jesus] had spit on his eyes, and put his hands upon him, he asked him if he saw ought"* (Mark 8:23). The man looked out of his once blind eyes and told Jesus that he could see but not clearly. (See verse 24.) So Jesus touched his eyes again, and the man's vision was completely restored.

As I read this story during my illness, I began to understand how Jesus was bringing wholeness to this man's soul. He was not simply healing his blindness. He engaged the man's *will*, for the blind man allowed Jesus to lead him outside of town. He engaged the man's *mind* by asking him questions, not to mention the questions the man must have asked himself about where Jesus was leading him and for what reason. Furthermore, the man probably felt many emotions, such as fear and hope—or both.

I wonder how this man *felt* when Jesus spat on his eyes? Was Jesus despising him, as others had? In one of his sermons, Kris Vallotton said that it was not uncommon for Pharisees to actually spit on people who were blind. They believed that blindness was a curse, brought on by that person's sin or the sin of his or her parents. So the Pharisees cursed the blind repeatedly by spitting on them as they passed.

Kris suggested that when Jesus used His own spittle in restoring sight to this blind man, He demonstrated that He had *reversed that curse*. This man, who had borne the shame and fear of being spat upon all his life, was experiencing the love of God through Jesus' action. Jesus changed the meaning of that once shameful act. And as the blind man's sight was restored, his deep psychological and emotional wounds were also healed.

As it was with this blind man, so it may be with you. It is a fact that some of the "wounding" experiences in your life cannot be changed. But Jesus' salvation works to restore wholeness to your soul by changing the meaning of those hurtful experiences. Every bad situation that has impacted your life and caused you *bitterness* can actually make you *better* when you allow Jesus to minister His wholeness to you.

One of the signs of your need for restoration may be a sense of confusion. You may have received a touch from Jesus; yet, like the blind man, you do not see clearly. When you are honest with God about your fear or other negative thoughts and feelings, you can expect to receive a second touch from the Lord. He will change your perspective, because your current one is keeping you from wholeness.

As you allow the Lord to touch your mind, He will change the way you perceive the people and situations that have harmed your mind. He gives you the grace to forgive your enemies, releasing them from your anger and you from your desire for revenge. Seeing life from God's perspective is vital to receiving healing and wholeness for your soul.

Some people are miraculously healed through prayer; others are healed as they see their need for the restoration of their souls. As with the blind man, Jesus may enter into a dialogue with a person seeking healing. He may have them examine themselves more fully and ask them to submit to Him in obedience. Whatever Jesus decides to do with us, we can trust Him to lead us by the hand and secure our wholeness, just as He did for the blind man.

Perhaps the most significant revelation I have received as I continue to study the soul's deep need for healing is the irrefutable fact that Jesus *wants* us to be made whole. He laid down His life to provide *sozo*, so that we could be truly free to walk in the abundant life He promises.

> **Jesus laid down His life to provide *sozo*, so that we could be truly free to walk in the abundant life He promises.**

What Does Freedom Look Like?

In the following chapters, you will read life stories of people who are experiencing *sozo* salvation—people who are rejoicing in the abundant life of deep peace and joy that Jesus has given them. These people have suffered many deep mental and emotional wounds in their pasts. Some of these wounds were caused by their own sin and wrong choices. Others were caused by people, especially significant others, who had sinned against them. But these sincere believers are being freed and delivered from their pain and are learning to walk victoriously in their divine destiny.

As I mentioned, Christians have settled for much less than what Jesus intends for them to enjoy. Too many people in the church today have become comfortable with platitudes, such as, "Sister, be encouraged"; "I feel your pain"; and "I'll say a prayer for you." When my pain seems unbearable, I don't want others to mock the promise of Jesus by telling me to be encouraged. If it is true that Jesus provides real deliverance and healing for me, I need you to help me find it.

Some have even taught that it is God's will for you to live in pain and distress, teaching that it will perfect your character and increase your humility. While it is true that *"all things work together for good to them that love God"* (Romans 8:28), we must remember why Jesus came. He came to deliver His people. He did not come to *encourage* the brokenhearted, the captive, or the bruised; He came to heal them and set them free. (See Luke 4:18.)

Healing for Your Dysfunction

Dysfunction is a term often used to blame someone else for our shortcomings, faults, and failures. Psychologists have promoted the idea that if the families we have come from were dysfunctional—i.e., not up to the norms set by psychologists for properly functioning families—we can blame them for causing all our problems. While dysfunction may describe the *fruit* of our problem, it does not describe the *root* of our problem. Sin is the problem; and the ugly fruit of dysfunction is the result of sin. Psychology has given us excuses for our failure; Jesus has given us a pathway to freedom.

> *Jesus does not encourage people in their misery; He came to earth to get them out of their misery.*

Indeed, Jesus does not encourage people in their misery; He came to earth to get them out of their misery. He died for this. He took all sin—every sinful thought, warped emotion, and rebellious way—upon Himself at Calvary. He intended for all of our perverted thoughts, emotional dysfunctions, and rebellious ways to be nailed to His cross, and for His blood to cleanse away not only sin but the very stain of sin.

Salvation to the Uttermost

As you discover the Holy Spirit's profound task of redeeming your soul, you will learn how He works *"in you both to will and to do of his good pleasure"* (Philippians 2:13). You need to know that He cares how you feel and how your wrong thinking defeats you. He has compassion on your broken heart, your captivity, and your bruises. He wants to heal you from the painful consequences of your sin, as well as pain caused by others' sin.

The Holy Spirit will show you His truth as it relates to restoring your emotional and mental well-being. He works in you to the end of restoring wholeness—salvation *"to the uttermost"* (Hebrews 7:25). The good news is that Jesus' salvation does more than encourage you with shallow words; He restores wholeness to your body, your soul, and your spirit.

I am convinced that when you truly believe Jesus' promise for you—abundant life in the way He offers it—you will step out of partial healing and into true and ongoing freedom. Your deepest needs will be met through His redemption. Your darkest secret will be expunged. That "one thing" in your soul that stands between you and the fulfillment of your destiny will be conquered.

THE "ONE THING" THAT HIJACKS DESTINY

I
t was a beautiful afternoon in Johannesburg, South Africa. I was teaching a series on prayer and worship in an outstanding church, founded by and built by students who were trained in our Bible college, Shekinah Bible Institute. It was so rewarding to see what this one couple had accomplished together in ministry. They shared with us that their lifestyle of prayer and worship, which we had taught and modeled for them at the Bible college, had been key to their success.

Tired from the morning ministry, I decided to take a nap before my next teaching. When I awakened, I experienced a strangely uncomfortable sensation in my fingers—a tension in the ligaments and a stiffness in the joints. I didn't think much of it at the time; I just continued on with my assignments.

As I traveled to Mozambique the following day, I had the opportunity to minister with another outstanding couple—Heidi and Rolland Baker.[5]

5. Rolland and Heidi Baker are founders of Iris Ministries in Mozambique.
Visit www.irisglobal.org for more information.

During this time, I began to develop an aching pain in both of my arms, as well. These symptoms continued throughout the next week as I ministered in the "bush bush" of Mozambique.

When I returned home to the US, there was still no relief from the pain in my arms. I went to my physician, who began a series of tests to determine the cause of my painful symptoms. However, no diagnosis was forthcoming, and, within a few months, the pain had spread to other joints. My hands and arms were becoming even more painful. Then I began to develop swelling in my legs and feet.

During the following months, I continued my schedule of ministry trips, still without a diagnosis. Then, while traveling, I suddenly lost the ability to stand or walk because of the pain in my knees. Devastated, I returned home in a wheelchair. I was hospitalized for five days and put through intensive testing to find the cause of my physical ailment and the possible treatment.

I had become so debilitated from these strange symptoms that I was only able to preach in a sitting position. It had been a year since I first started having the symptoms, and I had not yet improved. In fact, I had grown worse—much worse. I developed neuropathy in my feet, making it impossible for me to walk. And I had to start using a transport chair to go to church or out to dinner, and a small scooter to move around my home.

The constant, intense pain that I experienced during this entire ordeal drove me to God to find answers and healing from my illness. While I valued the knowledge that doctors could provide for my many conditions, they did not seem to have any answers for my current situation. They did not have a diagnosis, even after the many medical tests they performed. They could offer only treatments to alleviate the pain.

During my four decades of walking with the Lord, I have encountered various illnesses for which I have sought God for healing. Many times, He has revealed to me His will for all His children to be healed. And during the forty years prior to sickness, Jesus had always healed me of any ailments I had suffered. He had also healed others when we laid hands on them and prayed. Because of these testimonies, my faith had grown in His promise of divine healing. So this time was no different—I believed He would be faithful to His promises of healing.

But this journey proved to be different from those in the past, when I received answered prayers for healing. I would ultimately discover that Jesus wanted to do more than heal me physically. In the process of my physical healing, He would reveal to me how to be made *whole*—spirit, soul, and body. He was determined not only to *rescue* me from my physical illness but to *restore* my soul.

My Restoration Process

As I sought the Lord for my physical healing, He began to open up to me a world of understanding about the destructive forces we carry inside of our souls. These unhealthy fears, attitudes, thoughts, and emotions are detrimental to our bodies.

For months during this illness, the Holy Spirit began a process of restoring my soul. It was as if He began to peel away the layers of unhealed issues buried deep within my mind and emotions. He allowed me to see my destructive attitudes and mentalities as He saw them. And He showed me that they were caused by wounds in my past that had never been healed.

For example, I knew that I often adopt a survival mentality when I face difficult situations. I set myself up to get through them with a determination never to give up. To me, that was the key to success in my life, and especially in my ministry. I had suffered through some difficult and deeply disappointing situations during the years before my sickness, but I had survived. Wasn't that success?

It was as if the Holy Spirit said to me, "Not." Then He spoke this wonderful revelation to me: *It is not enough just to survive; you must be healed.* I began to understand that surviving is not the gospel. It is not the same as experiencing *sozo*, or being made whole—spirit, soul, and body. Surviving merely enables you to continue functioning, usually in an inferior level of *unwholeness*, in the face of life's mind-breaking challenges.

God wanted to "*sozo*" me—to rescue me from the destructive perils I had suffered in the past. He wanted to restore my mind to soundness and to give me His peace and joy. He showed me my need for healing from the inside out in order to make me whole.

It is not enough just to survive; you must be healed.

During the months I waited on God and struggled to find the key to my physical healing, my dear friend and colleague Dr. Sandra Kennedy spoke these enlightening words to me: "Sickness can enter through emotional pain just as it can through sin." She had learned this revolutionary truth through years of ministering in a powerful healing ministry.[6]

Until then, I had not understood that emotional pain could make me vulnerable to physical illness. I knew that sin could impede my pathway to healing, and I had asked the Holy Spirit to search my heart in that regard. He had showed me areas where I was not walking in the law of love, and I repented where I saw that I was falling short of that truth. Now, I began to open my heart to the Holy Spirit to show me my unhealed emotional wounds, which could be hindering my physical healing.

In the following months, I began to understand that I needed to be freed from my survival mentality. Based in a psychological wound, this unhealthy mind-set had caused me to coexist with emotional pain all my life. Along with the negative emotional responses it provoked in crises situations, this mind-set had ultimately become detrimental to my physical health.

A Low-Swimming Fish

I began to picture my survival mentality as a low-swimming fish, lurking in the darkness of my mind. Like the catfish, which is a bottom feeder in murky river waters, scavenging the garbage other fish reject, this unhealthy mind-set had invaded my psyche. It was always there, lurking just below the level of conscious recognition. It fostered a negative opinion of myself, and it triggered emotional pain when I faced challenges in relationships or other difficult life circumstances.

The catfish is not a difficult fish to catch once it is discovered; it is sometimes caught with bare hands. Its illusiveness lies in the fact that it chooses to hide in the depths of murky waters. This uncanny ability to remain hidden at the bottom of the river allows it to grow very large. For this reason, the catfish serves as a good analogy of the mental and emotional bondage we carry.

6. For more information on Dr. Sandra Kennedy and her healing ministry, visit https://www.sandrakennedy.org/healting-ministries/the-healing-center/.

We are often unaware of its origin or the strength of its negative influence in our lives.

When we suffer the "low-swimming fish syndrome," we actually begin to accommodate the pain caused by emotional wounds over time. We have felt the effects of our "catfish" garbage for so long that our psyches identify them as normal: "This is just the way I am; I always feel like this." These are lies that lurk in the murky waters of our minds, and they are used by the enemy to keep us in bondage. Without recognizing the problem and seeking healing for the one thing in our soul that holds us captive, we simply adapt to its presence. We accept its painful work and live our lives expecting to "always feel like this." The only way to break its hold is to catch it and expose it to the light of divine truth, setting us free from its ungodly influence in our lives.

Do you remember that when Satan approached Eve in the garden, the Scriptures describe him as the subtlest beast of the field? (See Genesis 3:1.) The Hebrew word for "*subtle*" in this verse means "prudent" and "crafty."[7] Like the low-swimming catfish, Satan is scarcely recognized in the dark, murky depths of our soul.

The Holy Spirit showed me that the enemy had found a hiding place in my psyche through which he could do his destructive work. His intent was to suppress my joy and victorious living, components of the abundant life Jesus died to give me. My emotional responses to Satan's work were not really based on what was happening that day. They were spawned by what had happened "yesterday"—the experiences that had wounded my soul and had not been healed and resolved!

> *"Sickness can enter through emotional pain just as it can through sin."* —Dr. Sandra Kennedy

Recognizing Your "One Thing"

In my years of ministry, I have observed many sincere believers who suffer from the "one thing"—an area of un-wholeness that continually prevents

7. *Strong's*, #H6175.

them from experiencing the abundant life that they seek. At times, they will seem well positioned to fulfill the divine destiny for which they are gifted. Then, the low-swimming fish that lurks in their soul begins to expel its garbage, impeding their freedom in Christ.

I have known ministers, for example, who have exhibited an ongoing struggle in handling their finances. Whether their financial decisions are influenced by personal irresponsibility or the darker threats of greed or dishonesty, they have terrible potential to thwart divine destiny. These ministers' otherwise stellar character and successful ministry suffers reproach from this "one thing" that they have never conquered and perhaps have never even acknowledged. If their unbiblical approach to handling money is broached by a mentor, they often dodge the conversation. Brushing it aside, they refuse to walk in the light. Unless they are made whole in this area, they will not escape the destructive power of their poor financial decisions.

Other Christians I have observed say they really want to be used by God to do His will, yet they oppose any thought of submitting their life to biblical patterns of authority. They do not recognize the need for genuine respect for pastors and other spiritual leaders. They do not grasp the significance of being a part of the body of Christ and allowing godly leaders *"to equip* [them] *for the work of the ministry"* (Ephesians 4:12 ESV). Though these sincere believers aspire to fulfill their God-given destiny, they allow this destructive, independent attitude to keep them from reaching it. They, too, need to identify the one thing that impedes their progress. They need to experience the freedom of being celebrated and supported in their calling by other members of the body of Christ.

These examples of the "one thing syndrome" could be multiplied, for there are many kinds of destructive forces that derail the godly pursuits of believers. As I mentioned, the salvation of our soul comes through a process of opening our hearts to truth and allowing our minds to be transformed by God's grace. The Holy Spirit is faithful to do His precious sanctifying work in our hearts as we continually yield to Him. He will empower us to obey God's Word in every area of our lives.

My journey through serious illness became an opportunity for the light of God to shine more brightly in the murky waters of my soul. God revealed the low-swimming fish that had caused so much suffering in my life and my ministry. Now it had gained ground in my physical body, by weakening my immune system's ability to fight the ongoing stress I was experiencing.

When the Body Says No

During those long months, several doctors had taken a stab at diagnosing my distressing physical illness and prescribing treatment to bring relief. Nothing worked. My body was still wracked with pain; my joints hurt so badly that I could not function. I continued to lose weight, and I was reduced to merely coping with an increasingly crippling condition. There seemed to be no end in sight, let alone a positive one. The more the doctors faltered, the more I knew that God was the only One who could answer my prayers.

About the time I began to explore the effects of my personal emotional wounds on my physical health, I came across a book entitled *When the Body Says No*.[8] My body definitely seemed to be saying no to any healthy response to treatment, so the title of this book captured my attention. I found it very helpful in assessing my current physical situation.

In summary, Dr. Maté's studies validate the idea that unresolved psychological conflicts and emotional pain do dramatically affect the immune system. The effects can be so serious that the immune system will give up its vital defense of the body. When that happens, an already present bacteria or free radical in the bloodstream can begin to work in our body.

Maté gave a number of examples of people who had become diseased and debilitated when their immune system simply let them down. In each case, the failure of the immune system to do its proper work could be traced back to specific periods of time when unhealed emotional wounds and unresolved psychological conflicts wrecked havoc in their lives.

As I read their stories, the Holy Spirit shined His light on my unresolved conflict, which, up to that point, I had been unaware of. Several years before the onset of my debilitating illness, I had suffered the loss of some very important relationships. I had consciously dealt with these losses by forgiving any offenses I had. And, as usual, I had survived and moved forward in my life and ministry.

8. Gabor Maté, *When the Body Says No: Exploring the Stress-Disease Connection* (Hoboken, NJ: John Wiley & Sons, Inc., 2011).

Recently, I faced another hurtful loss of relationships. I endeavored once again to forgive any offense, and my mind kicked into survival mode. This time, however, it was not long before my immune system shut down.

After months of inconclusive medical tests and sorely inadequate pharmaceutical remedies, I was referred to a medical specialist in Canada. He was familiar with the sudden onset of symptoms that I had experienced, and he had successfully diagnosed and treated many patients with those same symptoms, which were caused by the invasion of parasites. After testing me, he discovered that there were two types of parasites that had invaded my bloodstream and attacked my joints. Because my immune system had been compromised, these parasites were having their way in my body, causing the painful symptoms I had suffered for over a year.

Dr. Maté's book showed me the effects of a compromised immune system, as well as the possible causes. And my Canadian specialist had diagnosed my specific parasitic condition, which was treatable. As I put these good doctors' analyses and diagnoses together, I began to understand my pathway to healing. I realized that to enjoy physical health, it is absolutely necessary that I allow the Holy Spirit to heal my emotional pain. And I understood more clearly what my friend Sandra Kennedy had meant when she told me that disease could enter my body through emotional pain, as well as sin.

Along with submitting to the months of treatment to rid my system of the invading parasites, my new goal for restoring my health was to deal decisively with my low-swimming fish. I could no longer give place to the enemy of my soul by feeding my survival mentality. The Holy Spirit wanted to rescue me from this faulty mind-set. He wanted to redeem my soul from the need to survive emotional pain. As I learned to appropriate *sozo* salvation, the Lord became my Healer. Then the enemy no longer had a place of weakness where he could hide, creating stress that would rob me of my health.

He Sets the Bruised at Liberty

Because of the emotional and physical pain I suffered as a result of my low-swimming fish, I longed to receive the wonderful promise of Christ to *"set at liberty them that are bruised"* (Luke 4:18). I now understood that I was suffering from an unhealed wound in my soul—my mind and emotions. This bruise had taken away my freedom to walk in the abundant life Jesus came to give us. I rejoiced to know that Jesus' purpose was to set me at liberty from this long-standing problem.

The subtitle for Dr. Maté's book is *Exploring the Stress-Disease Connection.* He explained that we often respond to stressful situations, perceived or real, according to our personality and temperament. The way we respond to stress is often influenced by our family situations and the experiences that have formed our perceptions of life as children.

According to medical science, the human brain undergoes much development during early childhood, especially from birth to age five. The experiences we have during these years, positive or negative, play a foundational part in that development.

During the important formative years of my life, from ages three to five, I was separated from both of my parents. My older sister and I were placed into a children's home, and we did not see our parents for two years. Our mother was suffering from tuberculosis, and our father was an alcoholic—neither could take care of us.

This separation from the two most significant people in my life at that crucial age had a powerful impact on the development of my psyche. I began to understand that the emotional stress of my perceived abandonment by my parents spawned the development of my survival mentality. The loss of my parents, though only temporal, was traumatic; it created a wound that stayed with me into adulthood.

For me, loss of meaningful relationship as an adult still meant painful abandonment, similar to what I had experienced as a child. Gabor Maté explains how the vital relationship between the formation of our brains and the nurture we receive from our parents works:

> The disruption of detachment relationships in infancy and childhood may have long-term consequences for the brain's stress/response apparatus and for the immune system.[9]

---

9. Maté, *When the Body Says No: Exploring the Stress-Disease Connection*, 206.

Dr. Maté cites experiments that show a profound connection between early attachment disturbances and unbalanced stress-response capacities in animals. These same relationships exist in humans, as well:

> The crux of this research is that disrupted attachment in infancy leads to physiological stress responses in the adult.[10]

The loss of relationships that I suffered in the years and months before the onset of my illness triggered a stress-response that compromised my immune system. And because of that unhealed trauma from my early childhood, this relational pain stirred my mind and emotions, resulting in my "physiological stress response."

Later, Gabor Maté makes a startling statement: "Your pituitary is a better judge of your emotions than your intellect."[11] My low-swimming fish was not even recognizable to my conscious mind. But my pituitary gland, responsible for the fight-or-flight response, was aware of the subconscious pain that lurked deep in my psyche. So, after several painful emotional losses, it sent signals to my immune system to give up the fight. Deep inside my psyche, in the realm of my soul, an unhealed wound was saying to just give up—it was all too painful.

As a young child, I had made an unconscious commitment to the survival mode. That commitment, still functioning in my adult intellect, convinced me that if I was surviving life's painful situations, I was OK. On the other hand, my redeemed spirit and intellect were zealous to fulfill my God-given destiny; to be all God had called me to be. So, the "one thing" that could prevent me from walking in my destiny was the childhood wound that I hadn't yet dealt with.

I have shared my story as an example of why we need the *sozo* power of God to make us whole in every area of our being. There are places in our souls that need to be restored, or they will threaten our victorious walk with God. Hidden wounds will always color our perspectives on things. They will dictate the way we view ourselves, the people around us, and our life situations. As a result, we will not be able to confidently walk in God's will for our lives.

---

10. Ibid., 207.
11. Ibid., 268.

We may even lose the desire to continue such a painful journey toward our God-given destiny.

"He Restores My Soul"

Throughout the ages, God's will has been to "restore our soul." (See Psalm 23:3.) How comforting it is to read the prayer of King David after his great failure. You may remember how he committed adultery with Bathsheba and commanded that Uriah, her husband, be killed on the battlefield. When the prophet Nathan exposed his great sin, David realized his desperate need for divine rescue and restoration. In Psalm 51, we hear him cry out,

Have mercy upon me, O God, according to thy lovingkindness: according unto the multitude of thy tender mercies blot out my transgressions. Wash me thoroughly from mine iniquity, and cleanse me from my sin.
(Psalm 51:1–2)

Create in me a clean heart, O God; and renew a right spirit within me.
(Psalm 51:10)

Restore unto me the joy of thy salvation; and uphold me with thy free spirit.
(Psalm 51:12)

David confessed his sin and asked God to blot it out with His mercy. And he understood that his soul needed the *"joy of* [God's] *salvation"* (Psalm 51:12) restored to him. We can safely assume that he was disappointed with himself and his lack of character, which drove him to such heinous acts. How could he be healed from the unrest that came when, through his great folly, he had marred his own peace of mind? Though the Scriptures refer to David as *"a man after* [God's] *own heart"* (1 Samuel 13:14), that did not take away from his deep need of acknowledging his iniquity and his need for restoration. David needed to be cleansed from the effects of his low-swimming fish, which prompted his foolish and destructive actions.

What comfort saints through the ages have received from King David's heartfelt prayer! What a loss it would have been to David and to all of us if he had not cried out to God for the cleansing and restoration of his soul. Out of his agony, he gave to each of us the hope that we, too, can experience the restoration of our souls to righteousness, peace, and joy in the kingdom of God.

BEYOND RESCUE TO RESTORATION

I have always loved the biblical portrait of Jesus as the Good Shepherd, pursuing a straying sheep with great compassion to rescue it from certain destruction. One artist poignantly depicts Jesus leaning over a cliff to retrieve a frightened sheep.[12] Jesus said that His sheep hear His voice. (See John 10:27.) Who could be more grateful than the person who is unable to help himself when he hears the voice of the Good Shepherd and feels His strong, loving hands outstretched to rescue him?

It is important to understand that our Good Shepherd doesn't just *rescue* us from hopeless situations or from our personal issues. His purpose is to *restore* us to the abundant life He promised to give. I learned the hard lesson that merely adopting a personal survival mentality pales in comparison to living a life of freedom and wholeness. In fact, the stress that faulty thinking fosters is actually harmful to our soul.

---

12. Alford Usher Soord, *The Lost Sheep.*

The apostle Paul explained it this way: *"For this purpose the Son of God was manifested, that He might destroy the works of the devil"* (1 John 3:8). To *"destroy"* means to "loosen," "melt," "dissolve," or "put off,"[13] as in to set free or to discharge from prison. That personal prison can be ongoing depression, the hopeless inability to overcome temptation, or continual financial or relational failure. These and other works of the evil one in the believer's life are what Jesus came to destroy.

When Jesus rescues us, He intends to restore our souls so that we are no longer in bondage to the devil's work in our lives. As the Holy Spirit shines His light into the murky waters of our souls, we need not fear condemnation or accusation. Rather, as we acknowledge our desperate need to be rescued, He will lovingly cleanse us and set us free from our bondage.

As we acknowledge our desperate need to be rescued, Jesus will lovingly cleanse us and set us free from our bondage.

A Portrait of the Father's Love

Jesus' parable of the prodigal son (see Luke 15) is a beautiful biblical portrait of the heart of the Father to restore the soul.

In the story, a son demands his inheritance from his father. Somewhat surprisingly, the father complies with his demand. He allows his son to leave the family home, taking with him his portion of the family fortune.

The Scriptures say that the son went to a far country and *"wasted his substance with riotous living"* (Luke 15:13). He spent all he had and then got a job feeding pigs, which no self-respecting Jew would do unless they were desperate. He became so hungry that he had to eat the husks he was feeding to the pigs. Evidently, there was no person who would help him. (See Luke 15:12–16.)

In this destitute condition, the son remembered the abundance of his father's house, which even the servants shared in. He *"came to himself"* (verse 17) and decided to return home. His hope was that he would be rescued from starvation and that his father would accept him as a hired servant. He had a

13. *Strong's*, #G3089.

survival mentality. He rehearsed his humble speech to his father as he made his journey back to his childhood home. (See verses 17–19.)

How little did he perceive the love and compassion of his father's heart toward him, the wayward son. When his father, who had been watching tirelessly for his son's return, recognized him from a great distance, he ran to him and kissed him. I wonder if this rejoicing father even heard the prodigal son's speech, declaring that he had sinned against heaven and was no longer worthy to be called a son. (See verses 20–21.)

The Father's Awesome Gifts

As the prodigal son humbly poured out his carefully rehearsed words confessing his sin, his father interrupted him. He would not even listen to his son's surrender of his sonship in the face of his failure. Instead, the father changed the subject and issued commands to his servants, changing this prodigal's life forever:

> *The father said to his servants, Bring forth the best robe, and put it on him; and put a ring on his hand, and shoes on his feet: and bring hither the fatted calf, and kill it; and let us eat, and be merry.*
> (Luke 15:22–23)

The father, with his loving heart, could never settle for rescuing his son from starvation alone. Instead, he gave him gifts that signified his restoration to the family as an honored son. His *position* in the family was restored through the gift of a garment, which could be worn only by a son. His *authority* was restored through the gift of the family ring. (In that culture, the family ring was used as a seal in business negotiations and as a power of attorney.) And his sonship was established through the gift of sandals. In her book *God's Purpose for You*, Dr. Fuchsia Pickett explains the significance of these gifts:

> Sandals were a significant gift of the father to his son, for they represented his status of sonship. In Bible times, when someone was disowned and lost his sonship, he took off his shoes. Servants who were not sons did not wear shoes.[14]

14. Fuchsia Pickett, *God's Purpose for You* (Lake Mary, FL: Charisma House, 2003), 99.

What an incredible revelation of our heavenly Father's love. He loves us before we fail. He loves us during our emotional and mental struggles, and even in our rebellions. He does not love us less when we return to Him with the stain of our sin, needing to be washed clean. Our folly cannot diminish the Father's passionate love for us. As members of His precious family, we are ushered back into His world of blessing and abundance when we approach Him in simple, heartfelt repentance. There is no mention of survival status here; instead, our souls are restored to a greater likeness of our Father.

Our folly cannot diminish the Father's passionate love for us.

How can our heavenly Father be so magnanimous? He is so unlike us. And how can He actually restore His prodigal sons and daughters to such a place of respect and honor after their failure? It is because the Father's heart beats not just to forgive us but to reconcile and restore us to abundant life. He has no fear of us taking advantage of His love. The Father's heart is satisfied when we come to Him to receive His lavish gifts, which He delights to give us.

The Pharisee Spirit

The Pharisee spirit is a destructive enemy that deceives us into thinking we are not capable of being restored or of living in abundant life. It works closely with the spirit of condemnation, which tells us that we have failed too miserably to be restored. It also says that we are damaged merchandise and have lost all hope of fulfilling our divine destiny. It was this spirit that taunted the prodigal son as he returned home to face his father. The Pharisee spirit was exhibited by the elder brother in Jesus' parable of the prodigal son. He refused to forgive his brother, resenting all the fanfare the prodigal son received after returning home in disgrace. After all, the older brother reasoned, he had faithfully worked for his father the whole time, and there had been no such celebration for him.

Unfortunately, this uncompassionate attitude toward brothers and sisters in Christ who fail is sometimes seen in Christians today, who are working hard in the Father's house. Their faulty thinking convinces them that they can actually earn the love of the Father through their good works. They refuse to extend forgiveness to those who have failed in their eyes, deeming them less worthy than themselves, who are respected among the brethren.

This judgmental attitude hinders people from celebrating the restoration of sinners to the Father; it only condemns their failures. Many Christians have not clearly understood the magnitude of the Father's love and forgiveness. Indeed, it is contrary to our human nature to forgive. Without a revelation of the Father's heart, we will likely respond to believers who fail in the same way the older brother did in this parable.

How we need to understand our own humanity, which desperately needs the ongoing work of sanctification of the soul. If our attitudes toward others do not reflect the forgiving, loving heart of the Father, we have not yet experienced the wholeness that Christ died to give us. But in the restoration of our souls, we will experience the *"righteousness, and peace, and joy in the Holy Ghost"* (Romans 14:17) that characterizes the kingdom of God.

> *If our attitudes toward others do not reflect the forgiving, loving heart of the Father, we have not yet experienced the wholeness that Christ died to give us.*

When the revelation of the Father's lavish forgiveness and passion for our restoration finally breaks through to our hearts, we will experience freedom from the enemy who condemns us. And as we share the Father's joy in seeing our brothers and sisters restored, we will be delivered from the pharisaical heart of pride and unforgiveness.

The "Halfway" Forgiveness of the Pharisee Spirit

The pharisaical spirit engages in "halfway" forgiveness of those who have failed. In this way, it tries to hold back that person from progress, success, or emotional reconciliation. This ungodly mind-set would definitely hinder someone from rejoicing at the return of a wayward son, as the father rejoiced when he restored his son to the family with lavish gifts. And it would never celebrate fulfillment of destiny of an obvious failure.

At best, the pharisaical spirit will self-righteously offer a "halfway" for-giveness. It falls short of reaching restoration, and it demotes the person who sinned to a status of servitude, such as what the prodigal son asked his father to give him. King David became an example of this halfway forgiveness when he refused to let his son Absalom see his face.

After Absalom murdered his half-brother Amnon, he fled to refuge in Geshur, where he lived for three years. (See 2 Samuel 13:38.) Then, when he pleaded to return home, David relented, allowing Absalom to return to Jerusalem, but refusing to allow him to see his face.

Even though Absalom was home in Jerusalem for two years, living in his own house, he still yearned to be back in his father's good graces. When the pain became unbearable, Absalom demanded to see his father's face. He declared that he would rather be dead than continue living with his father's rejection. (See 2 Samuel 14:32.)

Finally, David allowed him to see his face, and he kissed Absalom when he saw him. (See verse 33.) Remember, the prodigal son's father kissed him, as well, running to him when he first spotted him on the road home. His for-giveness, represented in that kiss, was true and complete. Dr. Fuchsia Pickett shares with us the beautiful significance of the kiss of reconciliation:

> The father had been watching for his son, aching in his own heart because of the suffering he knew his son must be experiencing. Not only was the father watching for him, but he had gifts to give to him as well…The [first] gift of that kiss of reconciliation meant that everything was all right between them. The kiss is one of the most beautiful ways to express deep, intimate love. There is nothing on earth as wonderful as knowing that there has been reconciliation between you and your Father.[15]

Love that truly forgives does not give halfway acceptance, accompanied by conditional words and actions. To experience true restoration, the human heart and psyche require the intimacy of reconciliation that only comes through total forgiveness. Never forget that this is what Jesus died for—our complete restoration to wholeness—spirit, soul, and body. How many

---

15. Pickett, *God's Purpose for You*, 97.

psychological problems, how many emotional wounds and even physical illnesses stem from the inability of the human mind to deal with this pseudo-forgiveness, which is really no forgiveness at all!

Even after he saw the king's face, Absalom carried a deep bitterness toward his father, because their reconciliation was not complete. This offense must certainly have played a part in his eventual betrayal of King David when he tried to take the throne from him. Difficult family conflicts had left him with an unhealed emotional wound, which was never truly resolved.

How different is the portrait of our heavenly Father's heart, which is portrayed in the parable of the prodigal son? And what a different outcome there had been for the repentant sinner in comparison to his elder brother with his pharisaical spirit. We must carefully avoid the "little Pharisee" in ourselves that refuses to forgive others of their failure. Forgiveness, as demonstrated for us by God Himself, reconciles and restores relationships, fulfilling the destiny that God ordained for us.

> *Forgiveness reconciles and restores relationships, fulfilling the destiny that God ordained for us.*

Prostitutes and Tax Collectors Enter First

Jesus saith unto them, Verily I say unto you, That the publicans and the harlots go into the kingdom of God before you.   (Matthew 21:31)

The chief priests and the elders of the people were engaging Jesus in conversation one day when He went into the temple. Once again, they were questioning His authority to perform miracles and to make people whole. After reasoning patiently with them, Jesus finally rebuked them for their hypocrisy. The very people they despised as sinners, Jesus said, would go into the kingdom of God before them. What a thought! Publicans and harlots, people living in the depths of sin would go in before the religious people who prided themselves in keeping all the rules. How can this be?

Jesus' words show the true heart of God the Father and His passion for rescuing people to restore them to wholeness. What matters most is learning to recognize our need for restoration, which the religious leaders in this passage could not do. Instead, they chose to pursue their own righteousness, painstakingly dotting the i's and crossing the t's of their man-made rules.

Jesus demonstrated that those who are desperate to be rescued are better candidates for restoration than those who think they do not need to be rescued, those who are content in their faulty perceptions of themselves. For example, when the scribes and the Pharisees scoffed at Jesus for eating and drinking with the publicans and sinners, Jesus declared:

> *They that are whole have no need of the physician, but they that are sick: I came not to call the righteous, but sinners to repentance.* (Mark 2:17)

We might consider the response of Jesus to be tongue-in-cheek when he referred to the scribes and Pharisees as *"they that are whole."* That was apparently their perspective of themselves; they did not need a physician and felt superior to the sinners with whom Jesus was eating.

For example, when the scribes and Pharisees caught a woman in the act of adultery, bringing her to Jesus, they were ready to stone her for her sin, according to the Law. (See John 8:4–5.) Instead of suffering impending death, she simply gave Jesus another opportunity to demonstrate the way He rescues and restores our souls. First, He rescued her from the mob that was ready to stone her. He dispersed her accusers with the challenge, *"He that is without sin among you, let him first cast a stone at her"* (verse 7). And after saving her life, He made it clear that she did not have to continue in her sin. Neither would she have to live under the burden of condemnation from the pharisaical spirit. Jesus, the personification of the Father's heart of love and forgiveness, simply said, *"Neither do I condemn thee: go, and sin no more"* (John 8:11). With His loving rescue and words of forgiveness, He empowered her to be *restored* to a life without sin. And He set her free from the shame of degradation in which she had been bound. His words showed her that His plan was to set her truly free from her bondage, not just to rescue her life.

Jesus never ignored sin or condoned sinful behavior. Rather, He addressed it in a loving way, which showed the sinner there was hope of freedom from their bondages. People cannot be freed until they face the truth about who they are and what they have done. Jesus does not incriminate them when they confess their sin to Him. On the contrary, He releases them from the prison in which they are bound and begins to restore them to a life of wholeness.

> *Jesus never ignored sin or condoned sinful behavior. Rather, He addressed it in a loving way, showing the sinner that there is hope of freedom from their bondages.*

Jesus Restores Dignity

I don't think I had personally witnessed the restoration of dignity to individuals until I ministered in Mozambique. I ministered alongside Heidi Baker and her husband, Rolland, and I rode with their team on a flatbed truck out into the bush bush to preach the gospel. Among their team were young men and women who had been restored from the heinous crimes that were committed against them. Some had been physically defiled or even mutilated. I felt honored to preach the gospel side by side with those Spirit-filled believers, who had been made whole.

Now looking back, the poignant redemption stories of many people in that country bring tears to my eyes. Heidi told me of a young girl named Helena, who was forced to sell her body on the street in order to live. She only had one leg because the other one had been badly burned in a fire. Her grandmother, a witch doctor, told Helena's brothers to take her out into a field and kill her. She deemed her daughter useless because she had only one leg. They took her to a field and stoned her, leaving her for dead. But a Good Samaritan found her hours later, rescued her, and took her to a hospital where she received the medical help she needed to recover. When she got out of the hospital, she had to sell her body on the street to keep from starving. Due to her physical condition, she could only charge half of the fee other girls charged for their favors.

When Helena found out about Jesus, she accepted Him as her Savior, and it totally changed her life. She went back to her family to tell them that they could be saved, as well. Through Heidi's help, Helena was able to receive a prosthetic leg and walk again. Sometime later, Heidi officiated in the beautiful wedding of Helena to a young Christian man who loved her. She had been rescued from death, and she was walking into a life of wholeness that brought her into her eternal destiny and made her a minister of the gospel. Helena's days of living in a painful prison of prostitution and degradation were over.[16]

I love the word *over*. It is so wonderful to truly get past the past and walk into the future God intended for you when He made you.

Unlikely Companions

And certain women, which had been healed of evil spirits and infirmities, Mary called Magdalene, out of whom went seven devils, and Joanna the wife of Chuza Herod's steward, and Susanna, and many others, which ministered unto him of their substance. (Luke 8:2–3)

Especially to religious bystanders, Jesus seemed to be surrounded by unlikely companions. Mary Magdalene, for example, was known in the community as the woman out of whom Jesus cast seven devils. Yet we find her name listed among the women who traveled with Jesus and ministered to His needs—an unlikely companion for the sinless Lamb of God. Why would Jesus allow such companions to accompany Him? Because He knows that He can restore them to fulfill their destiny in His kingdom.

I have observed believers who have given up their personal self-esteem in order to maintain an unhealthy relationship they feel they cannot live without. Though they struggle with condemnation because of their choices, they feel that they cannot break free from their bondage. If they understood that being truly reconciled to Jesus would satisfy their emotional needs and allow them to keep their dignity, they could be restored to true fulfillment of their destiny. Instead, they convince themselves that they need certain relationships, which are detrimental to them. They are willing to settle for whatever makes them feel better about themselves for the moment.

16. Heidi Baker, *Compelled By Love: How to Save the World Through the Simple Power of Love in Action* (Lake Mary, FL: Charisma House, 2008), 81–83.

Feeling like you are a second-class citizen in the kingdom because of your personal bondage is never God's will for you. He wants to lift you up to a place of wholeness, where you can reign in His victory over the perverted mind-sets that plague you in any area of your life. When you have a poor opinion of yourself, you have not yet been made whole. And it is easy for you to believe Satan's lies that you are not good enough and that you don't deserve wholesome relationships built on mutual esteem.

Without seeking wholeness in Christ, human relationships become too important to us, and we strive to make people into what we need them to be to us—to meet our personal needs. When that happens, we find ourselves continually frustrated and disappointed when they respond to us poorly. There is no freedom in that kind of selfish relationship.

When I recognized my low-swimming fish, spawned by the separation from my parents as a young child, I realized that I expected too much out of my personal relationships as an adult. The Holy Spirit shined His light into my soul and showed me how I had looked to relationships to heal that childhood wound. I needed them to fill that empty place in my soul, which in reality could only be filled with that freedom and wholeness Jesus died to give me.

I began to understand that no person could heal the wound in my emotions and psyche. Only by looking to Jesus for the security and affirmation I needed could I be rescued and made whole in my soul. I wish I could describe to you the exciting freedom I experienced as I walked out of that personal prison. Now, as I look to Jesus alone for my emotional fulfillment, I am enjoying the abundant life He came to give me, and I am freer than ever to walk in the destiny that God ordained for me.

> *Only by looking to Jesus for security and affirmation can we be rescued and made whole in our souls.*

Jesus Satisfies Our Thirst

Jesus told the Samaritan woman at a well one day that He would give her the kind of water that would satisfy her so that she would never thirst again. Having had five husbands, and now living with a man who was not her husband, she still had a thirst in her soul that had not yet been satisfied. (See John 4:1–26.)

Have we even dared to dream that Jesus intends for us to be satisfied? I believe the enemy of our souls has deceived us with his lies of discontent. We have not considered Jesus Himself as the source of true satisfaction. And, like this woman who went from husband to husband, we go from one thing to another to find satisfaction for our souls, which only Jesus can give.

This promise of Jesus to satisfy the thirst of our soul is neither illusive nor difficult to attain. He told the woman in plain words that she had been drinking of the kind of water that could not satisfy her soul. (See John 4:13.) Then He declared that the water He offered her would be a well of water springing up into everlasting life. (See verse 14.) As their conversation continued, she learned the key to maintaining that reservoir of life-giving water. Jesus declared,

> But the hour cometh, and now is, when the true worshippers shall worship the Father in spirit and in truth: for the Father seeketh such to worship him. God is a Spirit: and they that worship him must worship him in spirit and in truth. (John 4:23–24)

When the woman asked how she could keep her new well of living water springing up to eternal life, Jesus took the time to teach her about worship. Worship brings you into His presence, where you can touch the fullness of His love for you. In that awesome presence, His life flows into you and gives you the abundant life He has promised.

When you continue to walk in a relationship of love and worship with Jesus, you allow Him to meet the deepest need of your soul. He then fills your place of emptiness, loneliness, or other painful areas of lack with His satisfying, divine presence. He takes the place of the friend you lost or the healthy relationship you never had with your parents or siblings. He fills the hole left in your soul from the rejection of others. Jesus heals the brokenhearted, as He promised He would; He sets them at liberty from their bruises and delivers the captives. (See Luke 4:18.) This is not a platitude. It is the relationship with God that brings wholeness.

This Samaritan woman's response to Jesus is that of one who truly desires restoration, not just rescue: *"Sir, give me this water, that I thirst not, neither come hither to draw"* (John 4:15). In other words, she was saying, "That's what I want. I receive what you are offering. I want to be rescued and restored to everlasting life by You, so that I won't go looking again to things that cannot satisfy."

Consider the dramatic difference between *rescue* and *restoration*. *Rescue* is when God's glorious hand reaches down and retrieves a lost sheep from destruction and death. *Restoration* is when He clutches that sheep to His bosom and supports him in his helplessness until he is made whole in Jesus' own love. The love of God rescues us from our failures; He restores us to fulfill our destiny.

Jesus doesn't take the yoke of failure off your neck to put a burden of condemnation on your back. There is life after failure. There is a future after you have wasted your opportunities. There is cleansing and restoration after yielding to temptation. The Redeemer of our souls is the God of second chances—and third and fourth chances. Even Old Testament saints understood the loving-kindness of God and His willingness to forgive. Consider these verses:

> But as for me, I will walk in mine integrity: redeem me, and be merciful unto me. (Psalm 26:11)

> Because thy lovingkindness is better than life, my lips shall praise thee. (Psalm 63:3)

Jesus doesn't take the yoke of failure off your neck to put a burden of condemnation on your back.

We Don't Know Ourselves

I have noticed a pattern in the way Jesus redeems our soul after we are born again. He knows that once we have been reconciled with God through faith in Christ, and our spirit is made alive to God, the process of restoration to wholeness has just begun. As I discussed, the Scriptures teach that the salvation of our souls is an ongoing process, involving the renewal of the mind, the healing of our emotions, and the submission of our wills to His.

It seems that God saves us and calls us to go and minister His grace to others first. And as we go, we begin to discover our need for wholeness. For example, Jesus called His disciples together and gave them power and authority to cast out devils and heal diseases. Then He sent them out to preach the kingdom of God and heal the sick. They succeeded in performing miracles and came back rejoicing—even the devils were subject to them! (See Luke 9.)

The love of God rescues us from our failures; it restores us so that we may fulfill our destiny.

Shortly after their return, they began to reveal their lack of character and their immaturity as they argued over who was greatest among them. (See Luke 9:46.) Then they informed the Lord that they forbade someone from casting out devils in His name because he was not one of them. (See verse 49.) And finally, they asked His permission to call down fire from heaven on the people of a village that did not receive them. (See verse 54.)

Jesus patiently continued His work of redemption in them, correcting each wrong attitude, emotional response, and perspective by showing them the love of the Father in each situation where they had failed. When they asked to destroy people who did not receive them, He told them that they did not know what spirit they were of, "*for the Son of man is not come to destroy men's lives, but to save them*" (Luke 9:56). These incidents show us that the disciples simply did not know the condition of their souls, even though they were following the Master.

Peter had a similar experience in receiving correction from the Lord when he developed a false confidence in his own courage and loyalty to Him. He was sure He would never turn from Jesus:

> *Peter said to Him, "Even if I have to die with You, I will not deny You."*
> *All the disciples said the same thing too.*　　　(Matthew 26:35 NASB)

All along, Jesus knew who Peter was and the redemption he needed in his soul. On one occasion, He told Peter that Satan had demanded permission to sift him like wheat. Then He added these incredibly comforting words, *"But I have prayed for you, that your faith may not fail; and you, when once you have turned again, strengthen your brothers"* (Luke 22:32 NASB). Still, Peter denied the Lord three times, cursing in the process.

Peter received a revelation of his low-swimming fish through his cowardly failure. It was in that dark moment that he realized his neediness, and he began to see himself as God did. He had to discover his false confidence in himself. His cowardice and unbelief had to be dealt with, or he could never fulfill the great destiny that God had planned for him. In order for Peter to become the amazing apostle that God called him to be, it was imperative that he recognize his need for wholeness and allow God to restore him. Only then would the enemy be denied a beachhead in him, where he could sift him and provoke continual failure.

Here is the wonder of it all: Peter's experience did not destroy him; it did not disqualify him from being a man of God. On the contrary, he was empowered to fulfill his destiny after he asked for forgiveness. Afterward, Peter was no less of a man than he was before; he became the man Jesus destined him to be. Through the restoration of his soul, his bitter failure became the launching pad that propelled him into his destiny.

Are you a candidate for the restoration of your soul? I am and continue to be. Whatever murky darkness abides in my soul, I want to expose it to the light of God's Word and allow the Holy Spirit to cleanse me. There are new dimensions of purity, liberty, and fulfillment of God's destiny in our lives when we receive greater measures of His restorative work in our soul.

As we yield to the Holy Spirit's redemptive work, we will come to know our heavenly Father in amazing new ways. He is a wonderful Father, who desires to deliver us from all spirits that separate us from His love.

> *As we yield to the Holy Spirit's redemptive work, we will come to know our heavenly Father in amazing new ways.*

4

REDEMPTION FROM THE ORPHAN SPIRIT

Heidi and Rolland Baker have rescued thousands of orphans in Mozambique. So when I heard Heidi say that the "orphan spirit" was the greatest hindrance to the church's fruitfulness, I listened carefully. And my eyes were opened to what has been an unnamed problem for pastors like myself, who desire to see believers firmly established in the love of God.

The Bakers have had a lot of exposure to the orphan spirit. When I traveled to their mission headquarters, I saw firsthand the expansive, redemptive work they were doing among the Muslim people. They have established thousands of village churches where precious Muslims, after observing miracles of healing, have turned to Christ and accepted Him as their Savior. Especially heartwarming was the Bakers' hands-on ministry called Iris Ministries, where they rescue thousands of children who are orphaned for a variety of reasons.

Many of these children have been taken into the mission's safe homes, to be cared for and educated. They have all come off the streets, where many learned to survive by selling their bodies for a morsel of food. They have had no one to care for them, no home or place of safety. Most of them became cunning thieves just to survive. The abandonment and mistreatment they have suffered have developed in them warped mentalities and defensive attitudes toward everyone.

Even though many children are accepted into a loving and caring atmosphere that Iris Ministries provides them, their survival habits are not immediately transformed. Many of them still exhibit negative emotional responses and a great distrust for people. For example, it takes them awhile to realize that they can eat every day without having to steal some food for their next meal. Their street cunning has taught them *not* to rely on anyone but themselves. These children anticipate human abuse and learn devious ways to avoid it.

A certain wariness pervades their every response to any overture from an adult. Accepting kindness in the past may have brought with it painful consequences. Can you imagine the questions in their minds as they receive Christian kindness? *Why would someone offer me these clothes? Why this bed to sleep in? Why this good food? No one has ever given me anything before without wanting something from me. What are they going to get from me in return? I'd better take this soap; it probably won't be here tomorrow.*

Trust has to be earned. With the survival mentality, the orphans do not trust in the love they are receiving, and it is not established in their minds and hearts in a day or even week. Only after experiencing the constancy of daily provision for their hunger do they begin to relax. And as their physical needs are met, along with receiving loving words and lots of hugs, these children begin to truly feel safe, at home, and loved.

Orphan: A Life Sentence

Orphan is a word that carries its own life sentence of loneliness, insecurity, inferiority, fear, and perhaps worst of all, a sense of being different and not fitting in with others. When I was in Mozambique, I attended an Iris Mission's outreach meeting one afternoon and found myself sitting beside one of the little girls from the Iris Ministries compound. I did not realize that some boys from the village were sitting behind us. I heard them speaking in a taunting tone to the girl beside me. My interpreter told me that they were telling her, "You're no good. You don't belong here with these missionaries. You're just an orphan."

Immediately, I put my arms around the child and drew her close. I said, "Tell them you're not an orphan any longer. You've given your heart to your heavenly Father. You are part of a great big family of believers who have also accepted Christ. You will never be alone again." After my interpreter told her what I said, she grinned up at me with a look of sheer gratitude that melted my heart.

The Divine Adoption Plan

As visitors to Iris Ministries, we were instructed *not* to refer to their children as orphans, even though they were orphans by definition, having lost both parents. But that is not who they *are* because they have been rescued; they are children of the family of God. And the pain of not having parents to care for them is gradually erased by the love and the care of their larger Christian family, who have taken responsibility for the raising of them.

I was deeply moved by the true work of redemption carried out in these children. They were rescued, not only from loneliness, poverty, hunger, and despair; they were now free from the stigma of worthless orphans, as well. They are valuable—precious children of their heavenly Father.

I wondered how many born-again believers need to receive this same personal revelation about themselves—that they are precious children of their heavenly Father. Perhaps they do not understand that when they received Jesus as their Savior, they were *adopted* into the family of God—elevated to the wonderful status of a son or daughter of their heavenly Father.

The Scriptures are clear that before we receive Christ as Savior, we are alienated from God and live as spiritual orphans. We suffer the painful consequences of that alienation in our entire being—spirit, soul, and body. The apostle Paul explains the wonder of our reconciliation with God when we are first born again:

*For ye have not received the spirit of bondage again to fear; but ye have received the **Spirit of adoption**, whereby we cry, Abba, Father. The Spirit*

itself beareth witness with our spirit, that we are the children of God.
                                                    (Romans 8:15–16)

But when the fulness of the time was come, God sent forth his Son, made
of a woman, made under the law, to redeem them that were under the
*law, that we might receive the **adoption of sons.***   (Galatians 4:4–5)

Various works of the Holy Spirit in a believer's life are sometimes described as the "offices of the Holy Spirit." They simply identify specific biblical functions of the Holy Spirit's redeeming work in the lives of believers. For example, Scriptures teach that He is the *"the Spirit of truth"* (John 16:13), whose task it is to guide us into all truth. He is described as *"the Spirit of life"* (Romans 8:2), giving us eternal life when we are born again.

Furthermore, the Holy Spirit also comes to dwell in the heart of believers, giving them *"the Spirit of adoption"* (Romans 8:15). He reveals to us that we are children of God, members of His family. He shows us that we are free from the orphan spirit that comes with our alienation from God. When we are born again, we become sons and daughters of the heavenly Father. That makes us eligible to receive all of the benefits of God's kingdom, including His abundant life, righteousness, peace, and joy offered through the Holy Ghost. (See Romans 14:17.)

When we truly understand that spiritual truth, our spirit cries out, "Abba, Father" (Romans 8:15). *Abba* is an endearing term used for our heavenly Father. It can be translated as "Daddy, God." The supernatural confidence that we are truly God's children is a result of the work of the Holy Spirit in our hearts, assuring us that we belong to Him. He reveals the heavenly Father to us and releases that loving cry in our hearts: "Abba, Father." As children of God, we can receive all we need for life.

> *When we truly understand that we are eligible to receive*
> *all the benefits of God's kingdom, our spirits cry out, "Abba, Father."*

Until we embrace this truth of our adoption into the family of God, we will behave like orphans. We will depend on our own wits to survive emotional and mental pain; we may even feel the need to steal from others to meet our own needs. Learning to depend on God as our Father involves being set free from the orphan spirit. As we receive this wonderful freedom, we realize our great privileges as sons and daughters of God.

In time, the Mozambican children who are rescued from the cruel life of orphanhood begin to relax and accept their new identity and their new Iris Ministries family. They refer to Heidi Baker as "Mom," and they know that they are free to go right into her house and help themselves to a Coke in the fridge. They have left their old identities as orphans behind and are walking in the freedom they now have as part of a *family*.

I observed some children there who were still oppressed by the orphan spirit. Though rescued by the Bakers, they stood outside in the yard and watched other children laugh and play. Distrusting their caretakers, they were afraid to even ask for what was freely offered to them, whether food or emotional comfort and acceptance. These children simply could not believe that they could have the same amenities and care that were being offered to the other children. They were still bound by the law of the orphan.

I realized what a perfect example these children's behavior was of the way some born-again Christians respond to the promises of God. They fall under two categories. Some believers freely and gladly enter in to all the blessings and promises of God. Others continue to live in fear and mistrust, walking in spiritual, physical, and even financial poverty. They still depend on their own wit to provide for themselves.

These sad Christians do not believe the promise of abundant life that Jesus proclaimed. (See John 10:10.) Instead, like spiritual orphans, they continue to stand outside Father's house, looking in. They are afraid to trust Him and afraid to take what they see Him freely offering to others. Their distrust and unbelief keeps them from responding to the Spirit of adoption. They have not yet learned that all they need to do is simply trust in their Abba, Father, and receive all they need from Him.

Believing the Lies of Satan

Heidi Baker's explanation of why some believers are not walking in the abundant life Jesus has promised comes from what she has observed firsthand of the orphan spirit. Many Christians simply cannot believe they are truly loved by God. They cannot grasp a love that gives them what they need, without cost. Instead, they believe the lies of the devil in opposition to God's truth.

Why don't born-again believers simply accept the provision of Calvary for abundant life and victory in every area of their life? The reason is quite simple: There is a wound somewhere in their psyche or emotions that opens them to Satan's lies.

The children in Mozambique have obviously been deeply wounded, and their minds and emotions bear these wounds. They have been abandoned and neglected by parents, either voluntarily or involuntarily, through death. The mind of a child has an innate awareness of its need for parenting, which is violated when he or she loses his or her parents. The subsequent mistreatment the child suffers at the hands of other adults deepens those wounds. This is how the traumatic life experiences of these Mozambican children becomes truth to them, making it hard for them to believe that any adult would love them freely and treat them kindly.

Similarly, the rejection or other wounding of our soul as Christians is not automatically healed when we are born again in Christ. As we discussed in that wonderful salvation experience, our spirit is recreated and we are placed in right standing with God by faith. (See Romans 5:1.) But Jesus understood our need for ongoing salvation, and He promised to send to us the Comforter—the Holy Spirit.

Jesus understood our need for ongoing salvation, and He promised to send to us the Comforter—the Holy Spirit.

The God of All Comfort

It is the Holy Spirit who guides us into all truth. He reveals to us the love of God through the Scriptures, and He renews our minds and fills us with the love of God as we yield our lives to Him. Jesus declared that the promised Holy Spirit would be our Comforter:

And I will pray the Father and he shall give you another Comforter,
that he may abide with you for ever; even the Spirit of truth; whom the
world cannot receive, because it seeth him not, neither knoweth him; but
ye know him; for he dwelleth with you, and shall be in you. I will not leave
you comfortless: I will come to you.　　　　　　　　(John 14:16–18)

Jesus promised that He would not leave us *comfortless*. The Greek word
that is translated *"comfortless"* is *orphanos*[17]—the basis of our word *orphan*.
The Holy Spirit is our divine Comforter, sent to us to redeem our souls. He
dwells within us as our Teacher and Guide; He is God's provision against the
orphan syndrome:

Blessed be God, even the Father of our Lord Jesus Christ, the Father of
mercies, and the God of all comfort; who comforteth us in all our tribula-
tion, that we may be able to comfort them which are in any trouble, by the
comfort wherewith we ourselves are comforted of God.
　　　　　　　　　　　　　　　　　　　　(2 Corinthians 1:3–4)

The dictionary defines the term *comfort* as "strengthening aid," "consola-
tion in time of trouble or worry," "relief or encouragement." Comfort is peace
and security. It is relief from pain or anxiety. It is a pleasantly relaxed state of
mind. It is like the sleeping cat on your lap that is spread out, with both ends
hanging over.

A crying child runs to his mother when he is hurt or hungry, because he
expects to find comfort. His mother doesn't need to produce a great, expen-
sive gift when he flings himself headlong toward her. She simply provides a
lap, two arms, a shoulder to lean against, hands that touch and soothe, and
a soft, loving voice. It is her comfort personified that quiets the sobs of her
son. Above all else, the responsibility of a mother or father is to provide security and protection that children can count on. Parents who do this become
human portraits of God's divine comfort.

One of Satan's powerful lies is that God will not comfort you; He will let
you down. Therefore, you need to watch out for yourself and shouldn't risk
disappointment by trusting God. To dispel the enemy's lies, we need to yield
to the work of the Holy Spirit in our hearts and minds. We must allow His

17. *Strong's*, #G3737: "fatherless," "parentless," "bereaved."

revealed truth to renew our minds so that we can receive the healing love we so desperately need to vanquish our orphan spirit.

Recovered Orphans

I was five years old when my parents came to the children's home to retrieve my sister and me. I can still remember many of my thoughts and feelings as I acclimated to life at home with my parents again.

For example, when my mother offered me a stick of chewing gum upon our return, I reverted to my orphan pattern of thinking. *At all costs*, I thought, *I must keep the rules.* So I asked mother incredulously, "You mean I can chew it in the house?" I clearly remember how tenderly she answered her "rescued" five-year-old. "Things are different in our house, Honey," she said with a loving smile.

It didn't take me long to realize that I could have things in my parents' house that were not available to me in "that other house." Here, I was not just one of many children being cared for in a way that necessitated an institutional approach. In my parents' house, I was their only baby girl. I could ask for things I needed—even for things I wanted. I never had to beg. And if the answer needed to be no, it was said kindly and often accompanied with an explanation.

When we are born again, we can expect to receive the same kind of treatment as loving parents give to their children. We can ask for things we need and even for things we want. Our heavenly Father's house is not like an institutional home where rules must be kept for the good of all. We can enjoy intimate fellowship with our Him as if we were His only child and have His full attention when we make requests.

> **When we are born again, we can expect to receive the same kind of treatment as loving parents give to their children.**

Recovery Programs

There are many people in our society who can benefit from recovery programs. They help many drug addicts and alcoholics, for example, break free from their bondages. To that end, specific recovery programs have become very popular in churches. Many are effectively ministering to people with specific needs.

But what about the believer who sits quietly in miserable bondage as a result of believing Satan's lies? What about those who have trust issues? What about Christians who do not yet understand that God desires a family into whom He can pour out His divine love? These hurting believers cannot grasp the truth that God the Father, the perfect parent, will never fail them. He will never forget to do what He promises, and He has promised to provide for their every need.

Jesus, our great Rescuer, comes into the lives of those who need "recovery" from unhealed wounds. He not only forgives our sins, but He also restores our soul so that we can be honored in the Father's house. That reality is what Jesus demonstrated in His parable of the prodigal son. (See Luke 15.)

No born-again son or daughter need be left outside of Father's house. No one should be found pining for His presence and wondering, *Does He really want someone like me near Him?* The answer to that question is an emphatic yes! Absolutely! Our heavenly Father really wants us in His house, freely enjoying all the promises He has made for our abundant living. He sent His Son, Jesus, to rescue us from the mess we were in and to bring us home to Him.

I mentioned earlier that Jesus promised to send the Holy Spirit, who would comfort us in every situation of life. Another Greek word Jesus used for the Comforter is *parakletos*,[18] which means, "one who is summoned to walk alongside, to give aid, to be an advocate for defense, to strengthen and help, to give counsel." What an amazing love! God the Holy Spirit dwells in me, walks beside me, helps me to receive the truth of God, and rescues me from the lies of Satan.

I vaguely remember one unhappy memory from the children's home that I could not understand when recalled years later. One day, I asked my sister, "Can you tell me if there was a room in the orphanage decorated in small black-and-white squares? I can't remember why those squares are lodged in my memory."

---

18. *Strong's*, #G3875.

With a kind smile, she plugged in the missing piece of that haunting puzzle: "Those were the black-and-white tiles you stared at during times you had to sit on the bench for misbehaving." She continued, "You spent so much time there that I felt sorry for you, and I climbed up on the bench and sat beside you."

My big sister's compassion is just a small glimpse into the compassion of the Holy Spirit, who stands beside us in our darkest moments. Jesus kept His promise to give to us the Holy Spirit, the divine Comforter, and did not leave us orphans. When we choose to believe His truth instead of the enemy's lies, we can rest in the truth that we have a heavenly Father who loves us. We have an elder brother—Jesus—who is our Savior and constant friend. And the Holy Spirit is always with us to keep us from feeling alone. The triune God will rescue us, even from those shadowy black-and-white-tile memories that represent misery long forgotten.

God doesn't simply provide divine comfort by what He does for us or what He gives to us; God *becomes* our comfort, because of who He is. In the story of the prodigal son, the father wrapped his strong loving arms around the prodigal. He kissed him. He rejoiced and expressed his joy for the return of his son to his heart and home. This is who God *is*. He is a deeply feeling Father—the epitome of a caring parent—and His love never gives up on us. His love never fails!

> *God doesn't simply provide divine comfort by what He does for us or what He gives to us; God becomes our comfort, because of who He is.*

Foregoing Sibling Rivalry

In His desire to give believers abundant life, God has indeed made many great and precious promises to us. Though He lavishes His attention upon us, we need to understand that we are not the only children. We are part of the body of Christ, the family of God. So, while we want to be freed from an orphan spirit, we also need to recognize the value of our brothers and sisters in Christ, as well.

Unfortunately, Satan works hard to disrupt the familial unity after he has lost the battle of convincing us we are orphans. He will try to draw our attention to what other believers have received, their gifts and abilities. He brews envy and jealousy in us over the things they are able to do that we cannot. He whispers to us that if God loved us as much as He loves His other children, He would do the same for us.

If the devil can stir jealousy in our hearts, he will foster a "performance spirit" to create unhealthy competition between us and other believers. God does not promise to give all His children the same kinds of blessings. Not all of His children will have the same kind of ministry or the same beautiful family that we all admire. Just because we are all part of God's family does not mean we are entitled to everything other Christians have.

God has purposes for destiny, special gifts and callings and even divine encounters that are different for each believer. Just as Joseph's brothers were jealous of the coat of many colors given to him by His father, we, too, can sometimes become jealous, wanting the blessings we see that others have received. The enemy of our soul delights in promoting our discontent. In doing so, he causes us to lose sight of the blessings God has given us and the destiny He has given us to fulfill.

At the root of this deception is the orphan spirit. Because the orphan spirit does not relate to a father's love, it does not trust the loving character of God. It measures His goodness by the things He gives or does not give to them. When we are released from the orphan spirit, we understand that God is for us, with us, and in us to do good for us. Also, when we realize that we have the favor of God in our lives, we do not need to grapple for the favor of man. We believe that our heavenly Father loves us simply for who we are, not for what we achieve or for how we stand in other peoples' evaluation. We are free to believe, as Heidi Baker's children, that the Father truly wants us in His house; He wants to give to us every good gift He has chosen for us. We understand the declaration of apostle James that *"every good gift and every perfect gift is from above, and cometh down from the Father of lights, with whom is no variableness, neither shadow of turning"* (James 1:17).

When we receive this wonderful revelation of the Father's heart of love for us, His children, it sets us free from the torment of the orphan spirit. As His children, we can expect Him to continue His redeeming work in every area of our souls that we surrender to Him. He doesn't just put a bandage on our profound wounds or inborn iniquity. He eradicates them, because they are poisonous to our soul. And He pours His oil of healing truth over them, so that we are made completely whole. Let us bow in worship to Him forever because we are no longer orphans.

PRESCRIBING A PILL FOR
AN EARTHQUAKE

Have you ever heard someone in your church make these kinds of observations about visitors: "They would make a good family for our church," or "I hope they decide to come to our church; we could use some people with their gifting"? Well, why wouldn't you want to receive into your church those mature Christians who can help fulfill the vision that God has called you to accomplish? As a pastor, I understand this natural desire to have people join us in reaching our vision, people who can make a difference and help us to fulfill the destiny to which we are called as a church.

But what about the harvest—the hurting people who don't have a clue about destiny, purpose, or God's love? Isn't that why the church exists, to bring people to Christ and to see them established in His love and purpose for their lives?

Recently, a very loyal couple in my congregation shared with me that they had invited a troubled family to our church who did not know the Lord.

My natural instinct first caused me to think, *It will be a real challenge to bring them to the Lord and to help them to be healed and set free.* It is easy to think about how needy people will affect *us* when they show up in our lives or in our churches. Fortunately, my next thought was more redemptive: *This is the harvest. This is what it looks like. It is every person without Christ and hurting souls representing a myriad of needs for redemption.*

Is it any wonder that we don't see the harvest? We may see people we are hesitant to help because of our own reluctance to commit to the daunting task ahead of loving them into the kingdom, or even our legitimate feelings of inadequacy.

What did Jesus see when He said, *"Lift up your eyes, and look on the fields; for they are white already to harvest"* (John 4:35)? Jesus saw people who desperately needed the salvation—*sozo*—that He had come to earth to provide for them. He told His disciples—and to each of us—to lift up their eyes. Sadly, the harvest was all around them, but they didn't see it. Do we?

Beggars on the Steps of the Church

In Acts chapter 3, we read of an event that involved religious people who had forgotten—or perhaps never knew—why they were religious. It is a story of a lame man who was carried every day to the temple steps to beg for alms. He was there to receive the help of compassionate people who passed him on their way to the temple to pray.

When Peter and John went to the temple during the hour of prayer, their response to this lame man was unlike anything he had ever heard before:

> *Then Peter said, Silver and gold have I none; but such as I have give I thee: In the name of Jesus Christ of Nazareth rise up and walk.*
>
> (Acts 3:6)

After Peter's startling declaration, he actually took the lame man by the hand, lifted him up, *"and immediately his feet and ankle bones received strength"* (Acts 3:7). Then the lame man began to walk and leap and praise God. (See verse 8.) Before Peter came that day and offered the man *sozo*, the religious people had helped the man a bit by giving him alms. But that was not what he really needed. He sat helplessly as a beggar on the church steps to receive his most basic needs for survival; no one expected that his real need could be or would be met.

The bondage that kept this crippled man from living a normal life was accepted by all as incurable. The thought that he could become a whole and functioning member of the church never entered the minds of the good religious people. They felt satisfied with themselves just for giving him a few coins. Offering hurting people so little when they need so much is what I like call "giving them a pill for an earthquake."

> *To offer hurting people so little when they need so much is like giving them a pill for an earthquake.*

Giving People the Right Stuff

Because those who need healing are just as convinced that their healing is impossible as those who pass them by, they may be like the man on the temple steps—content to ask for alms in the place where healing should be happening. After all, someone was kind enough to carry him to the steps every day. But extending kindness is much different than extending *sozo*. Kindness looks with pity on the poor and needy for their plight; *sozo* deliverance breaks their chains. The power that heals the needy harvest is much greater than kindness. No longer can we be content with carrying needy people to the steps of the church. Giving them a few coins will not suffice. It is time to tell them what they really need and to help them receive the complete redemption that Jesus promised.

The lame man did not need silver and gold as much as he needed his health. When his health was restored, he could earn the silver and gold he needed. Peter and John had faith that would heal him through the name of Jesus. They gave him what he really needed.

Here is my question for the church: How much longer will the church let lame men and women sit on the steps of the church, receive a little kindness, and then go home in the same pitiful condition in which they came? Perhaps unbelievers have lost their belief in the power the gospel to change lives. They watch as believers carry those who are crippled around, year after year, helping them eke out a meager existence. Maybe they even admire our kindness to support the lame in their misery. But they are not impressed with the way the church works with hurting lives. Unbelievers are not amazed when they see people carried to the church steps to beg for alms. In contrast, when Peter and John gave the lame man the *sozo* deliverance that Jesus had provided for him, the people were all amazed. (See Acts 3:10.)

> *Unbelievers are not amazed when they see people carried to the church steps to beg for alms.*

What Would Jesus Do?

Jesus was amazing. Just reading about His normal daily activities is cause for true admiration. For example, when Jesus encountered Mary Magdalene one ordinary day, He cast out her devils. (See Luke 8:10.) Then she began to accompany Him on His daily mission trips. When He rescued the woman caught in the act of adultery, He loved her back to life, forgiving her and giving her a second chance. (See John 8.)

Another day, He met a man at the pool of Bethesda and asked him, "Do you want to be made whole?" (See John 5:6.) And on an ordinary day in the life of the Lord, that man vacated that pool forever. (See John 5:9.) And who can forget the *sozo* experience of the Gadarene demoniac whom Jesus set free? When his neighbors found him, he was clothed and in his right mind, sitting at the feet of Jesus. (See Luke 8:35.) And because he was set free, he also wanted to follow Jesus.

As Christian leaders and sincere believers, we must recognize how much we have to learn about offering true salvation—meaningful and relevant deliverance to tormented souls all around us. I am not suggesting that we are failures if not everyone is physically and spiritually healed as we minister to them. But I believe it is fair to say that we need our level of expectation raised to receive the supernatural life Jesus came to give us. And then we need to share that supernatural life with others. For many, this is a far cry from "doing church as usual."

Every person should have the opportunity to learn about and receive wholeness—*sozo*—the complete salvation that Jesus died to give us all. I am saying that when we direct people toward an experience with Jesus to experience His deliverance, they can expect a deep and radical change in their lives. He has given us authority and commanded us to do what He would do to bring His kingdom to earth.

> *God has given us the authority and has commanded us to do what He would do to bring His kingdom to earth.*

The Secret of the Church's Power

When we read of the supernatural power and explosive expansion of the early church, it is apparent that those first believers were plugged into something that many people in our churches have missed out on. When we read about these believers living a life of continual prayer and fellowship, teaching and sharing their lives with one another in love (see Acts 2), it seems like a dream that is too good to be true. Perhaps that is why many leaders and believers today associate miracles with early church only.

In fact, as I have taught on this passage in the book of Acts, I have related this description of the early church to what we call "revival" in today's church. If we are honest, it fills us with amazement that Christians actually lived this lifestyle. They were focused on only loving and serving Christ, reaping the harvest as He had commissioned them to do on the earth. Their priorities and activities in life were centered on allowing the power of Christ's salvation to manifest itself in their lives and churches.

We have so many different ideas today about what church is. Unfortunately, many have lost the thread of the gospel that teaches us how God intended His church to function: as an organism that heals and restores lost souls. Instead, the church today models a cleverly packaged and smooth-running organization. Many leave out of their practical theology entire sections of the apostles' instructions to the churches. It is no wonder, then, that we find ourselves inadequate for the task of ministering to those of the harvest, performing the miracles of salvation that they need.

For example, the Epistles of Paul teach the biblical model for ministry and corporate church life. They give us an idea of what our missing link is to experiencing and offering to others the *sozo* power of the gospel. Paul taught that God gave gifts to the church to establish His kingdom in the earth:

> WHEN HE ASCENDED ON HIGH, HE LED CAPTIVE A HOST OF CAP-
> TIVES, AND HE GAVE GIFTS TO MEN....*And he gave some as apostles,*
> *and some as prophets, and some as evangelists, and some as pastors and*
> *teachers, for the equipping of the saints for the work of service, to the*
> *building up of the body of Christ.* (Ephesians 4:8, 11–12 NASB)

In the apostle Paul's epistles, he includes several lists of spiritual gifts, including gifts of healing, working of miracles, prophecy, and so on. (See 1 Corinthians 12, 14.) And he lists gifts of teaching, giving, ruling, mercy, etc., to edify the body of Christ. (See Romans 12.) Each of these spiritual gifts is a precious divine empowerment to establish the kingdom of God on the earth. They equip the saints to harvest the souls that Christ died for.

The gifts Jesus gave to the church of apostles, prophets, evangelists, pastors, and teachers are distinguished from other divine gifts. They represent individuals whose lives are called and expressly anointed for the responsibility of equipping saints to do the work of the ministry. (See Ephesians 4:11–12.) These "people gifts," which are sometimes referred to as the fivefold ministry gifts, are used by men and women who are committed to the body of Christ and who live faithfully before God to fulfill their divine calling.

It is important to understand the divine purpose for these "people gifts." The responsibility of these men and women is to equip believers for the work of the ministry God has called them to do on the earth. Every Christian needs to be a part of a local church that is equipping them through biblical teaching and that provides role models who carry out the purposes of God in the church, like reaping a great harvest of souls.

Too often, because those with God's "people gifts" are not functioning in the church, many believers who would make wonderful reapers do not understand their purpose of bringing in the harvest. Without this focus, I believe, the church has resigned itself to a less than powerful existence. We have not made a real difference in bringing *sozo* to our communities, changing our culture. Instead, many are content to carry the beggars to the church steps. They hope someone will give them a little bit of help—like offering a pill for an earthquake.

Remember the Gadarene demoniac. He was so grateful to Jesus for his deliverance that he wanted to leave everything and follow Him. Jesus made it clear that the best way for him to show his appreciation was to go tell others of the great things Jesus had done for him. (See Luke 8:39.) He was made whole by the Master, and he was equipped to share the good news of the gospel with others. This is what ministry truly is. When we are healed and restored, we show our gratitude to the Lord by sharing the same redemptive experience with others.

> *This is true ministry: When we are healed and restored, we show our gratitude to the Lord by sharing the redemptive experience with others.*

Keeping the Main Thing the Main Thing

As Christian leaders, it should be unthinkable to allow believers to remain in bondage to their past wounds and failures. We should empower them to experience the freedom Jesus came to give through complete salvation. We need to seek God for power and understanding on how to equip them to do the work of the ministry. Only in doing so can we obey Jesus' injunction to *"heal the sick, cleanse the lepers, raise the dead, [and] cast out devils"* (Matthew 10:8).

It is important to keep the main thing the main thing. For too many, the command of giving freely what we have freely received is one we don't yet have a handle on. But if life was freely given to us, why on earth don't we contend for the release of God's love and power to freely give it to others? We cannot afford to let the enemy hold us back through fear and confusion any longer while we watch our homes, communities, and nation fall under the power of his destructions.

The Danger of Forgetting the Main Thing

During my recent illness, I experienced my first (and hopefully my last) visit to the emergency room at the hospital. I was experiencing tachycardia, a very rapid heartbeat. I realized I needed immediate medical attention to determine its cause and to rectify the problem. In that alarming situation, you can imagine my consternation with the formalities I encountered upon my arrival at the hospital. I became exasperated with the questions like, "What is the name of your insurance company?"; "Have you been here before?"

I am normally a fairly patient individual, and I was trained by my mother to act like a lady at all times. But desperation kicks the sides out of our carefully constructed "proper behavior" boxes. I interrupted the next question that was mercilessly hurled at me (as it seemed to be). I felt that, in that moment, I was the only one who understood the extreme urgency of why I was there.

"Listen to me a minute," I pleaded, keeping my voice as calm as my rising alarm allowed. "My heart is beating out of my chest. I need your help. Do something! I don't want to answer any more questions."

In my physical distress, I did not have the tiniest bit of interest in their record-keeping information. I did not care about the hospital's mission statement, the nurse's name, or even that of the hospital director. I wanted someone to alleviate my possibly life-threatening distress. In simple terms, I wanted to scream, "Somebody, help me!" I wanted them to keep the main thing the main thing: my pounding heart needed attention.

When people come to lay at the steps of our churches, do we tell them about our missions' program, our children's ministry, and our next building program, or do we treat their "pounding heart?" Are we addressing the main thing they need, attentive to their inside scream, *Won't somebody just help me?*

If we truly understand the purpose of our ministry, we will wait on God to empower us for the equipping of the saints—restoring, repairing, perfecting, binding up—until they are free to do the work of the ministry and until they zealously desire to give freely of what they have received. That's what it means for the body of Christ to keep the main thing the main thing.

FREEDOM THROUGH FORGIVENESS

Marla hated her alcoholic father. And naturally, she had every reason to hate him. In his drunken rages, he regularly abused her mother while she and her siblings hid, clinging to one another, terrorized by his violent temper. In short, Marla's father had destroyed her family's home.

One day, when she came home from school, Marla found her mother crouching in a corner, wiping a mixture of blood and tears from her face. As Marla surveyed the room in disbelief, she saw the soup that had been cooking splattered everywhere in the kitchen. What had been their table and chairs was now a pile of painted wood splinters strewn throughout the room. The ax her father had used lay nearby.

Marla's shock registered on her face as she stared at her mother. "Your daddy—" her mother managed to whisper through her sobs, "flew into a rage, beat me, and then chopped the table and chairs into pieces. I couldn't do anything to stop him." Putting her face in her hands, she continued to sob quietly.

It had never occurred to Marla's mother that she could leave her husband. How would she survive? She knew she couldn't support her family without his paycheck. At least he put food on the table. Though she worried for the safety of her children, she did not know where she could find help.

Marla was overwhelmed with her mother's fear and helplessness. She had seen enough. She had watched her mother and siblings endure enough. This anguish had to stop. A frightening resolve filled Marla's heart to end this recurring nightmare.

Hiding a pistol under her mattress, she planned to end her father's life when he returned. Surprisingly, he did not come home that night—or the next. On the third day, when she decided to inspect her carefully hidden weapon, she discovered that it had disappeared. She never found it again and never knew what became of it.

Fast-forward Marla's life ten years later. She has accepted Christ as her Savior and is a deeply committed Christian. Finding His forgiveness and love, Marla wants nothing more than to please God with her every breath. But her daily struggles remind her that there is still a deep anger within that disturbs her peace. It comes from nonspecific origin; she can't identify the source of it. Yet it relentlessly rises to the surface, causing her to react angrily in situations, especially those in which domestic violence is mentioned.

One day, as Marla sat in our Sunday service, she heard me tell the story of my father's alcoholism and its negative impact on our home. And aside from his devastating problem, I described my father as a talented man, fun and exciting. As she listened, Marla began to ponder, *How is it possible that Sue can speak of her father in such kind and respectful terms?*

Marla wondered, *How can she remember him in that way after he caused them so much pain on a regular basis? After he abandoned her and her family? Why is it that she doesn't resent him as I resent my alcoholic father?* It was then that the Holy Spirit revealed to her the source of her deep-seated anger. Marla had heard me. She recognized the power of forgiveness working in me that had healed the pain caused by my troubled father. And she acknowledged her ongoing hatred of her father.

Marla was perplexed. She continued to think: *Is it is possible to be freed from this ball of hatred I hold in my heart toward this man—even after he caused my mother and my whole family such unspeakable grief? If so, how?* Marla began to pray and asked the Holy Spirit to show her the answer to that terrible question. And His answer came so simply and clearly, "Yes, it is possible. Sue forgave her father. That is why she is free."

Marla's first thought in response to what she heard was, *My father is the one who did this to our family. How can it be that I am the one who is responsible to make it right by forgiving him?* She even wondered, *Does God really know how awful our suffering has been? Surely, if He did, He would not require me to forgive my father.*

Forgiveness: God's Inexplicable Gift to Us

For anyone who has suffered at the hands of another, Marla's initial response was normal. The unfairness of the treatment she received and the pain it caused rankled inside her. Likewise, when we are hurt, we ask questions like, "Why do I have to make it right when they are responsible for the wrong? Why doesn't God deal with them?" These and similar questions are often the universal response when we are told that it is our responsibility to forgive someone who has hurt us deeply.

What Marla would soon begin to understand is that forgiveness is actually God's inexplicable gift to us. Forgiveness is more beneficial to us than to our offender. When we choose to forgive an offense, we are set free from the victim mentality that allows the offender to be in charge of our emotional responses for so many years—sometimes even for life. We are set free from anger, resentment, bitterness, and other destructive mental and emotional forces when we choose to forgive. And as God gives us grace to release our captors, who have caused us such deep emotional distress, we are free to walk into our destiny without hindrance.

The Holy Spirit began to show Marla that forgiveness is the only true power against the evil that had been inflicted against her. It is *because* men are evil and inexplicably cruel that God has provided forgiveness through the power of Christ's redemption. Forgiveness is our means of escape—a gift to set us free. By forgiving our enemies, we are set free from bitterness and disallow negative emotions to destroy our lives.

> *By forgiving our enemies, we are set free from bitterness and disallow negative emotions to destroy our lives.*

It is simply a fact that the venom of hatred and bitterness, though spawned by the offense of one person, affects a lot more than the victim and his or her situation. If they are not dealt with through the power of forgiveness, these powerful negative forces will continue to afflict us, surfacing in other areas of our lives. Hatred and bitterness can gain such strongholds in our minds and hearts that they can affect our entire lives.

What Makes Forgiveness So Powerful?

What makes forgiveness so powerful? How can it be the greatest gift and most powerful weapon we have been given against our destructive emotional wounds? Because when we forgive, we are placing those who have hurt us into God's hands. We are, in a very real sense, releasing our deathlike grip around their necks, demanding revenge and punishment for the pain they have caused us.

Sometimes people think that if they forgive an offense, it means they are condoning it, excusing it, or even justifying it. That is not true. To "forgive," by definition, means "to give up resentment of or claim to requital for [a suffered grievance]." Forgiving our offender means letting go of the offense. It means releasing our offender from our demand for revenge or justice. We no longer act as their judge and jury.

Instead, when we forgive, we simply appeal our legal case to our loving Savior. In that place of surrender, when we repent of those negative emotions toward our offender, we are set free. We are free from the power of the offender, which continually victimizes us through those destructive emotional responses within our soul. We disallow any further offense to invade our thoughts and emotions. In that simple, though often difficult, decision to forgive our captor, we enter into a place of freedom, where the divine healing power of God can wash us and make us whole.

Through our forgiveness of offense, we are able to receive the reality of Jesus' purpose for coming to earth. We allow Him to heal our broken hearts and deliver us from our captivity to emotional and psychological pain. (See Luke 4:18.) Who would dream that one act of our will could foster such profound change? When we choose to forgive, the Holy Spirit begins to work powerfully, though invisibly, on our behalf to take away the pain, heal our wounds, and set us free from their invasion of our lives.

Why We Struggle

Since forgiveness is such a wonderful gift that sets us free from crippling pain, we could wonder why we struggle to forgive. Part of the answer is that carrying unforgiveness has become a way of life for many people. The devil's work is to deceive us. He does not want us to understand that the grudges, resentments, and hatred we hold on to are curable diseases. They can all be cured by forgiving the perpetrator of our "disease." There is no other way—only by choosing to forgive offense can we be cured of our emotional bondages.

Unfortunately, some people's emotional responses have been formed in the womb of bitterness. For example, many have grown up in an environment where hearing bitter and critical comments about others is the norm. It does not occur to them that these negative attitudes and words are wounding their psyche.

If you grew up in a family where your parents and siblings yelled and screamed at one another, you may think that every family yells and screams the way yours does. Because no one ever apologizes or asks forgiveness for their bad behavior, this ranting becomes acceptable to you; you see it as normal way to communicate.

Perhaps you have read about the bitter feuds between the Hatfields and the McCoys, real family clans who lived in the Appalachian Mountains. They argued over everything and threatened each other continually. There were several murders between the families; revenge became the watchword between the two clans.

Why didn't someone stop the insanity? Why were their children taught to be loyal to their clan and to hate the other? Someone has given us an amusing picture of their plight, saying, "An eye for an eye, everybody goes blind." There is no end to the madness and mayhem as long as grudge-holding and vindictiveness continues through generations.

I am acquainted with a person who is a descendant of the Hatfields. She told me there is a story about the leader of the Hatfields who earned the name Devil Lance because he was such a cruel man, a murderer. By God's mercy, the day came when he gave his heart to Christ and was born again. My friend said that the preacher who baptized him jokingly said that he had "baptized the devil." Yet, as a result of his true conversion, the cycle of hatred and revenge that had passed down from generation to generation and ruled his family began to break.

Until someone breaks the cycle of hatred and revenge, unforgiveness will destroy families through generations. Within a "screaming" family, it is common for children to grow up, marry, and continue the cycle of screaming at their children. Some have admitted to me that that they wonder why they scream at their children whom they love. T. D. Jakes described this destructive cycle in graphic language: "Clinging to generational unforgiveness is as foolish as drinking poison and waiting on someone else to die."[19]

Clinging to generational unforgiveness is as foolish as drinking poison and waiting on someone else to die. —*T. D. Jakes*

Release from Hopelessness

The day that Rosemarie Claussen was born, her room was filled with exquisite bouquets of exotic flowers. Because Rosemarie's father was a general in Adolf Hitler's SS elite corps, it was appropriate to celebrate the birth of his daughter by congratulating this very powerful man. After all, she was to be named *the goddaughter of Adolph Hitler*. Because of her father's celebrated status, Rosemarie would be a child of extreme privilege—wealthy, highly educated, and living the posh life of a young German royal.

---

19. T. D. Jakes, *Let It Go! Forgive so You Can Be Forgiven* (New York, NY: Atria Books, 2012), 63.

Then calamity struck her family. Her honorable father disagreed with Hitler's diabolical agenda and refused to be involved in the atrocities of the Holocaust. That is when everything changed. Rosemarie's father was forced to take a poison pill; her mother and Rosemarie and her siblings were fortunate to escape the same fate. As they ran for their lives, they hid in a forest for days to avoid their would-be captors. They slept in a chicken coop and lived on scraps they foraged for their meager meals day after day. Rosemarie became filled with hatred and bitterness; inwardly she hated the man—her godfather, Hitler—who had turned her life and her family members' lives into a living hell.

Her clothing tattered, her body broken, Rosemarie sat and stared in bewilderment, not wanting to know what she looked like. Hot tears streaming down her face, she put her fist into her mouth to stifle her sorrowful screams, as she thought about the many ways she wanted to see her tormentor suffer. Then she groaned and cried out, "Nothing is cruel enough to repay him for his wickedness. My life is ruined. My family is destroyed. There is no hope. Evil has overcome us!"

Rosemarie desperately needed a powerful medicine to cleanse her psyche of the poison of unforgiveness and revenge. The unthinkable evil she desired for this tormentor had become a monster in her mind. Thankfully, just as "Devil Lance" Hatfield did, she discovered the love of Jesus and experienced forgiveness for her sins, and the peace of God filled her soul. With that discovery, she received the medicine that cured what had seemed to be, up to that point, an incurable grief. She was introduced to the incredible gift of grace, which enabled her to forgive her tormentor for his unpardonable offense.

As Rosemarie received the grace to forgive, to release her tormentor from her terrible judgment, she found that her own heart was released from captivity to hatred. She was no longer a victim of violent, negative emotions. Rosemarie became a victor in life and began to move forward, pursuing God's wonderful destiny.

The most powerful result of forgiveness is that it brings healing and restoration to our deepest wounds, so that life can begin again. It enables victims who have been caught in the vise of hatred and rage to be released from their private hell and to enter a world of peace and joy, usefulness and productivity.

The most powerful result of forgiveness is that it brings healing and restoration to our deepest wounds, so that life can begin again.

Rosemarie and her husband established a ministry center in Sweden for pastors who need a time of refreshment and restoration. I have traveled in ministry with Rosemarie and her husband and have been privileged to teach at their international center in Sweden. I learned that they often used their own financial resources to bring weary pastors from former Communist countries across the Baltic Sea to their center. These wounded warriors are taught about the power of forgiving their enemies; they experience healing from betrayal and heartache similar to what Rosemarie experienced.

I remember standing and gazing across the Baltic Sea and being thrilled at the profound, divine love that had empowered the Claussens to reach into those Baltic countries. Theirs is a ministry spawned by the freedom of forgiveness they had experienced—the remarkable work of restoration that had occurred in Rosemarie's heart through the power of forgiving her enemies.

In retrospect, Rosemarie understood that this precious gift of helping others experience freedom through forgiveness had been made possible by her personal pain. She tells her story in her book entitled *Tears Turn to Diamonds*. It is a story of triumph over the devastating cruelty that made Rosemarie and her family victims of hatred and cruelty.

Forgiveness Is a Medicine

Forgiveness is not a dutiful command to cause you misery or hardship; it is a medicine that cleanses you from the poison of unforgiveness. An honest look of the biblical view of forgiveness moves us to consider where our real problem began. It helps us to acknowledge it and then to deal with it in a biblical way, bringing resolution to our ongoing pain.

Consider the word *victim*. It refers to someone who is "injured, destroyed, or sacrificed under any of various conditions." When we feel like a victim, we are held forever in a destructive state of mind, with no way out. There is a hopeless aura that surrounds a person who feels victimized by a harmful force in life; it translates into "once a victim, always a victim." In the natural, you cannot change your status once you have become a victim of tragic or harmful situations. But God does not connote hopelessness to our lives, no matter how degrading the torment we have suffered.

Though the word *victim* is not found in the Bible, even born-again Christians have been deceived into embracing such a mentality. They live their lives under a dark shadow of the excruciating pain, feeling like a hopeless victim of a person or circumstance. According to God's Word, we are not victims without hope; we are simply people *who have been sinned against.* In that regard, we need a divine cure from this mind-set. And the therapy God has provided to heal our deepest psychological and emotional wounds is *forgiveness*—the act of setting free the one who offended us.

> *We are not victims without hope; we are simply people who have been sinned against.*

Jesus takes the guesswork out of how to live in freedom. He taught clearly that He came to give us abundant life (see John 10:10) that is filled with peace (see John 14:27) and joy (see John 15:11). So, when He taught us the principles of forgiving our enemies, it was not to burden us with an impossible task. He knew that we could not be free to live in peace and joy as long as we harbor malice and unforgiveness against someone.

When Peter asked Jesus how many times he had to forgive a person who sinned against him, he offered his own reasonable calculation: *"Till seven times?"* (Matthew 18:21). Jesus' response must have confounded him with its obvious hyperbole: *"I say not unto thee, until seven times: but, until seventy times seven"* (verse 22).

Then Jesus told a story to illustrate His point that there should be no limit placed on our forgiving attitude:

> *Therefore is the kingdom of heaven likened unto a certain king, which would take account of his servants. And when he had begun to reckon, one was brought unto him, which owed him ten thousand talents. But forasmuch as he had not to pay, his lord commanded him to be sold, and his wife, and children, and all that he had, and payment to be made.*

The servant therefore fell down, and worshipped him, saying, Lord, have patience with me, and I will pay thee all. Then the lord of that servant was moved with compassion, and loosed him, and forgave him the debt. But the same servant went out, and found one of his fellowservants, which owed him an hundred pence: and he laid hands on him, and took him by the throat, saying, Pay me that thou owest. And his fellowservant fell down at his feet, and besought him, saying, Have patience with me, and I will pay thee all. And he would not: but went and cast him into prison, till he should pay the debt. (Matthew 18:23–30)

In Jesus' story, the king, when informed that the servant whom he had forgiven such a large debt had treated his own servant in a cruel manner, threw him into prison and demanded full payment of his debt. Of course, the servant's dilemma was hopeless, since there was no way for him to make a payment while he was bound in prison.

Then Jesus explained that our plight is equally hopeless *"if* [we] *from* [our] *hearts forgive not every one his brother their trespasses"* (Matthew 18:35). We can easily relate to having such a great debt, for we were only forgiven when we accepted Christ's payment for our sins. At Calvary, Jesus laid down His life to purchase our redemption, so that we could experience peace with God and the abundant life He offers us. If we, in turn, do not forgive those who have sinned against us, we are like the servant who was forgiven such a great debt but demanded the payment of his fellow servant.

In the story of the Hatfields and the McCoys, we concluded that when we demand "an eye for an eye, everybody goes blind." In Jesus' story, He illustrates how unforgiveness imprisons everyone. The man who cannot pay his small debt to his fellow servant is a prisoner, and so is the servant whom the king forgave but who refused to forgive the debt of his fellow servant. Jesus said that the unforgiving servant was delivered to the tormentors in prison. (See Matthew 18:34.) Hatred and revenge in the soul becomes a cruel prison.

Forgiveness is the key that unlocks prison doors and sets everyone free!

A Change in Mentality

It is a mystery of amazing grace that when we release unforgiveness, we set our offender free from our desire to punish. And, in turn, we are set free from the judgment of God for the unforgiveness that we hold in our hearts. Forgiveness is the key that unlocks prison doors and sets everyone free! As Rosemarie Claussen discovered, forgiveness is the key to breathing the rarified air of psychological freedom. It is an open door to a new life—a meaningful life—pursuing your destiny with a heart filled with love for other hurting people.

If we understand the heart of the Father toward those who need forgiveness, our unforgiving mind-sets will be changed. Often, in our victim mentality, we think, *How unreasonable it is to ask me to forgive such a great wrong.* But in the light of Calvary, God's heart says, "How perverted your thinking is, considering the great debt you have been forgiven."

As we focus on what Jesus did for us on the cross, we begin to understand how huge our debt of sin was. Only the death of the Son of God could purchase our forgiveness. When we consider that we have been forgiven all of that debt, it will become reasonable to our minds to forgive the small offenses and sins committed against us. And as we humble ourselves before God, choosing to forgive, we will experience His grace that empowers us to do so.

Jesus said that offenses will come. (See Matthew 18:7.) The Greek word for "*offense*" used in this passage is *skandalon*,[20] which means "trap" or "snare." It is closely related in meaning to the word *scandal*. The enemy brings offense into our lives to cripple our emotions with hatred, bitterness, resentment, and other destructive responses. He intends to kill and destroy our God-given potential. (See John 10:10.)

If we don't evade the trap of offense through the redemptive power of forgiveness, we will truly become victims of the hurts we have suffered. It matters not to the enemy what situation or experience he uses to trap you in the destructive power of unforgiving attitudes. One offense is as good as another to accomplish his evil purposes in your life.

When you yield to the Holy Spirit's work and embrace unlimited forgiveness toward your offenders, you spring the trap set to ensnare your soul.

---

20. *Strong's*, #G4625.

As you do, forgiveness will become a way of life for you, renewing your mind with the law of love found only in the Father's heart. And you will learn to live in the rarified air of divine freedom offered to you in the kingdom of God—the righteousness, peace, and joy of the Holy Ghost. (See Romans 14:17.)

In the next chapter, we will consider the *process* of forgiving devastating offenses that have deeply wounded us. Simply mouthing words of forgiveness, no matter how sincerely, may not immediately set you free from your bondage. Sometimes you may need to grieve your losses. But it is well worth the journey to live in the freedom of the kingdom.

HEALING FOR
THE WOUNDED SPIRIT

As children, many of us chanted the familiar adage, "Sticks and stones may break my bones, but words can never hurt me." We were taught this little saying to show our invincibility to the jeers and taunts of other children. Perhaps to children who mainly understand pain as only a physical discomfort, this proverb holds some truth. However, to adults who understand the misery of psychological and emotional pain, it becomes a self-deceiving proverb. We know that words do indeed have devastating power to hurt. The book of Proverbs addresses this truth:

> *The words of a talebearer are as wounds, and they go down into the innermost parts of the belly.* (Proverbs 18:8)

Of course, words are not the only source of deep psychological wounds, as I discovered from my childhood abandonment by my parents. Wounds result from the unloving behavior of others toward us, such as discrimination and the violation of our person, whether it is physical, verbal, or emotional.

Entire people groups have been oppressed by governments that are prejudiced against a certain race or religious sect. And unhealed wounds created by such oppression spawn bitterness, distrust, fear, and sometimes irrational responses of individuals or entire societies toward authority. A wounded person views all of life through the prism of his or her own painful experience, which is sometimes the result of prejudice toward them for simply being of a different race.

In a previous chapter, I shared with you my deep childhood wound, caused by losing my parents at a young age. During the years my sister and I spent in the orphanage, I was too young to understand my wounded spirit. But, as I grew up, I found that my mind-set, which had been unconsciously shaped by the abandonment, could affect my entire emotional paradigm of adult relationships.

We have discussed how a physical wound that is left untreated can set the stage for infection, which adversely affects the whole body, and which sometimes has fatal consequences. Similarly, untreated psychological wounds can have devastating effects on our emotional and mental health.

Wounds, whether physical or psychological, don't just fade away. They must be treated appropriately to ensure that the body and mind can regain health and then maintain that health. It is this understanding of the human mind that led to the science of mind and behavior—psychology—as well as the mind's disorders—psychiatry.

In more recent years, following the wars in the Persian Gulf, Afghanistan, and Iraq, our nation has become all too familiar with the post-traumatic stress disorder (PTSD). This syndrome characterizes many soldiers, along with others, who have experienced traumatic situations and require *treatment* to restore them back to health. PTSD therapy is just as imperative as the care needed to mend physical injuries that occur on the battlefield.

Two Major Causes of a Wounded Spirit

Several years ago, I was invited to observe Carlos Annacondia's ministry in Argentina. This passionate evangelist is credited with bringing revival to

Argentina. He has won over three million people to Jesus, and he has seen thousands of people, in both his nation and other nations, freed from many kinds of mental and spiritual bondages. I felt privileged to learn under him and to gain a deeper understanding of the power of *sozo*—supernatural salvation and deliverance.

When I learned that, according to their careful follow-ups with new believers, 80 percent of converts from Annacondia's crusades become established Christians involved in local churches, I was amazed. My research had shown that in our nation, only 5 to 10 percent of converts from large crusades remain committed Christians. So I questioned him on how such a large percentage of his converts become fruitful Christians through his ministry.

In explanation of this apparent phenomenon, he responded, "In American evangelistic crusades, you invite people to come to Jesus to be born again. That is good. But in our crusades, we offer them not only the assurance of eternal life in Christ; we pray with them to be set free from spiritual bondages so they are empowered to live a victorious Christian life."

Annacondia shared that he had discovered two main causes of a wounded spirit—*trauma* and *rejection*. He explained that *trauma* seemed to damage the human mind in a way that it disorients the person and allows the devil to take advantage of their mind, filling them with fears and tormenting thoughts.

Similarly, *rejection* devastates a person because it violates their deepest need—to be accepted and loved as a person of value, or to belong. A person suffering from rejection will often be driven to find emotional comfort anywhere and at any cost of their dignity and well-being. The wound of rejection and its companion, the fear of rejection, often unconsciously motivates a person to engage in destructive relationships just to feel accepted.

As we discuss these two major wounds of the mind, I encourage you to ask the Holy Spirit to reveal any area of your life that might be affected by such a wound. He will gently reveal the source of pain you have suffered through trauma or rejection or both. By addressing these psychological wounds, you will begin to enjoy the wholeness of *sozo*-redemption that Jesus came to give to you.

The Wounds of Trauma

Carlos told me a deeply moving story about Maria. Her deliverance was truly amazing. As a nine-year-old girl, Maria was sexually abused by her father and was forced to watch him sexually abuse her sisters, as well. The sickening scene was repeated before her eyes day after day, and Maria could no longer bear the emotional and mental anguish she and her sisters were suffering. Inexplicably, Maria began to go blind.

When she attended one of Annacondia's crusades, she asked him for prayer to restore her eyesight. Blindness had been healed in their crusades, and he prayed with faith for Maria to be healed. Nothing happened. So he stopped to ask her some questions and was informed of her home situation and the pain that she suffered. The Holy Spirit revealed that her psychological pain was the cause of her blindness. She was going blind because she could not bear to watch the horrific abuse occurring in her home.

Annacondia instructed Maria that she needed to forgive her father and release him from her hatred and bitterness. He told her that Jesus would help her to do that, and then he led her in a simple prayer. As Maria sobbed, praying a prayer of forgiveness of her father, her vision miraculously returned!

Psychologists have long observed this phenomenon of hysterical reaction to trauma. People have been known to lose their sense of feeling, their hearing, or the use or their limbs due to the physical response to trauma. As the enemy took advantage of Maria's nearly insane state of mind, she actually became blind.

The Wounds of Rejection

In addition to trauma, the second major cause of a wounded mind is *rejection*, perceived or real. The deepest need of our mind is to be accepted and loved for who we are. God made us this way so that we live in relationship with Him and find total satisfaction in Him.

Unfortunately, sin intervened and distorted that desire, causing mankind to turn from God and to seek satisfaction in other people and things. We became vulnerable and suffered pangs of rejection in relationship with other fallen people. Sin separated the entire human race from the true source of love: God, our Creator.

When Jesus came to restore our peace with God (see Romans 5:1), His mission was to heal that deepest sense of rejection: our innate need to relate to our Creator—Redeemer. When we are born again, we are reconciled to God's love, which is able to satisfy the deepest need of our hearts. As we yield our lives to the Holy Spirit, we begin our journey to wholeness. He reveals to us areas of un-wholeness—wounds in our minds that need to be healed.

Charlotte began her journey to wholeness many years ago when she received Christ as her Savior. As a young girl, she watched as her parents drove away, headed to the golf course, as they did almost daily. Golf and other social activities filled their lives and their time. Leaving Charlotte and her sister home alone did not seem selfish to them; their girls would be there when they returned.

There was a meaningless exchange between Charlotte and her parents each day as they left: "We won't be very long, honey; try not to miss us too much. Just be glad you're rid of us for a while so you can do what you want to do."

Charlotte wondered if they were trying to cover a sense of guilt as they joked lightly about the pursuit of their obsession—golf. It seemed that their golf buddies were eminently more important to them than their daughters' need for quality time with them. "Oh, take your time. I thought you'd never leave today," Charlotte would laugh weakly, as she played along with their joking.

All the while, she was trying to cope with their seeming lack of interest in her. She desperately tried to hide the inexplicable pain she felt. Many times, as Charlotte watched them drive away, she would run into the house and dissolve into sobs, sometimes even into screams of anguish. The truth she perceived was that her emotional needs were not as important to her parents as their social involvements. But she did not realize that it was the pain of rejection that broke her heart, day after day.

As a child, what could she do? Could she say, "Wait! I need you to love me, spend time with me, show that you care"? If she asked them not to go, her instincts told her that she would be forcing them to show that they cared. She was convinced that if they *really* cared, they would want to take time to spend with them. Nobody wants pretend love.

While Charlotte's mother was affectionate with her at times, her father seemed to live in his own world. He seemed oblivious to his daughters' presence, except to occasionally correct them. She couldn't remember a warm, gentle caress or loving word from her father that affirmed her as a girl or the beautiful young woman that she was becoming. She would soon begin to search for that vital affirmation elsewhere, in less than healthy relationships.

To be sure, the human mind becomes desperate for the missing affection and affirmation it legitimately craves. Charlotte was no exception. As soon as an attentive teenage boy began to pay her special attention, she felt that she had discovered a remedy for her emptiness and loneliness. When she was with him, it seemed that her emotional pain would subside.

When her companionship did not seem enough for him, Charlotte began to fear that she might lose him. He was all she had to assuage the pain of her loneliness and rejection. So when he threatened to end their friendship if she continued to refuse his physical advances, Charlotte acquiesced. It was the first of step toward the path of compromising her high moral standards—all in an attempt to heal the pain of her rejection.

Years later, after happily marrying and starting a family, Charlotte received Christ as her Savior. She began to serve God with all of her heart. However, as she tried to put childhood memories behind her, she discovered that she still harbored a deep wound from the rejection of her parents. She still believed the lie that there was something wrong with her that made her parents reject her.

It is natural for a person who suffers rejection to ask, "Why did they reject me? Am I not good enough? Can I ever measure up? If people don't love me, how can God love me?"

Rejection wounds the psyche deeply, keeping a person from understanding their value. It robs them of their personal sense of worth. Charlotte was caught in this paradigm of rejection as an adult. Though living a godly life, she still found herself constantly trying to earn her sense of worth by serving God. This caused her to make faulty comparisons between herself and others, who appeared to be more valuable than she was. It became unbearable for Charlotte to be in situations where she felt that someone else's talents or abilities were preferred over hers. It only strengthened her belief that she just did not measure up—once again.

These feelings of inadequacy open the door to the destructive forces of jealousy, fear, and insecurity, which add to the struggle of rejection. A person who has much to offer can actually sabotage their success by acting out of their insecurity and jealousy, which thwarts healthy relationships. What a cruel enemy we have, who wins twice—first by inflicting the child with pain of rejection and then by using that unhealed wound to rob them of their destiny.

The Lasting Effects of Trauma and Rejection

According to the Scriptures, mankind was not given the ability to cope with a wounded spirit:

> *The human spirit will endure sickness; but a broken spirit—who can bear?*　(Proverbs 18:14 NRSV)

The human mind was simply not built to sustain a wounded spirit. If we have been deeply wounded and have not received healing for our soul, our pain won't just go away over time. The maxim "time heals all wounds" is simply not true. The truth is that only Jesus can profoundly heal our souls, and He came to undo the destructive work that Satan has worked in our lives: *"For this purpose the Son of God was manifested, that He might destroy the works of the devil"* (1 John 3:8).

> *Only Jesus can profoundly heal our souls, and He came to undo the destructive work that Satan has worked in our lives.*

In my personal situation, the trauma I suffered as a young child, and the perceived rejection by my parents during their duress, had wounded my psyche, which remained that way well into my adult years. I did not realize its ongoing devastating effects at the time; I simply considered every disappointment in my adult relationships to be another abandonment. I was unaware that this unhealed wound from my childhood had resulted in my serious lack of coping skills as an adult.

As I explained earlier, many Christians misunderstand the redemptive work of salvation in their lives. They think that accepting Christ as our Savior automatically heals all psychological hang-ups. It is true that we become new creatures in Christ the moment we are born again. (See 2 Corinthians 5:17.) We have peace with God (see Romans 5:1), and our spirit is reconciled to God, who is Spirit.

But what about life here? The Scriptures show us that when we are born again, we do not become completely Christlike in our thoughts, desires, and ambitions. The apostles teach throughout the New Testament that our *minds* must be renewed and transformed (see Romans 12:2), our *emotions* must be cleansed or sanctified by the love of Christ (see Ephesians 5:25–26), and our *wills* must be conformed to God's will through continual surrender to Him (see Romans 12:1).

> *Our minds must be renewed and transformed, our emotions must be cleansed by the love of Christ, and our wills must be conformed to God's will through continual surrender to Him.*

In our journey toward wholeness of the soul, the Holy Spirit will begin to expose those destructive strongholds that keep us from being made whole. I believe every person has a God-given desire within to experience the real freedom that God created us for and then redeemed us for. I think this longing is demonstrated in the words of the psalmist:

> *As the hart panteth after the water brooks, so panteth my soul after thee, O God....Deep calleth unto deep at the noise of thy waterspouts.*
> (Psalm 42:1, 7)

Like the deer, desperate for a drink of water, our soul cries out to God to make us whole. And it is the Holy Spirit who identifies and reveals to us our deep need, so that we can be healed.

Soul Ties That Wound the Psyche

There are other sources of psychological wounds besides trauma or rejection. Other wounds occur through unhealthy soul ties created in significant relationships. Before we became Christians, many of us had developed natural attachments to people, tying our thoughts and emotions to their approval, disapproval, and other opinions they'd had about us. Apart from the divine influence of the Holy Spirit, these attachments are influenced by the fallen world and even the enemy of our souls. In many ways, these emotional attachments can destroy our minds.

Soul Ties in Families

Deep emotional bonds are normal in family relationships. However, when separated from God's love and purposes, they can conceivably destroy a person's life. A fascinating story found in the book of Genesis suggests that inordinate soul ties exist even within legitimate family relationships.

The Old Testament patriarch Jacob had twelve sons. However, his two youngest sons, Joseph and Benjamin, were his favorites. So the older brothers decided to separate Joseph from their father. Their fierce jealousy motivated them to sell him into slavery and then convince their father he was dead.

Years later, during a terrible famine, Joseph's sons had to travel to Egypt to find food. But they were unaware that the ruler of Egypt in charge of giving them food was their younger brother, Joseph. Without revealing himself as their brother, Joseph demanded that they bring Benjamin to Egypt.

His brothers begged for mercy, knowing that their father, Jacob, would grieve himself to death if anything happened to Benjamin. They said that *"his life is bound up in the lad's life"* (Genesis 44:30). The favoritism Jacob showed these two younger sons reveals that, though he was a beloved patriarch of Israel, his family relationships were inordinate. His love was not distributed evenly between his older sons and his two younger sons.

When do normal, loving emotional bonds among family members become destructive? The answer to that question differs from one situation to another. However, you can suspect an unhealthy soul tie if your whole life revolves around a child, a parent, or another family member.

If you realize you cannot be happy or at peace unless your family members are functioning in the exact manner you desire, you may be exhibiting an inordinate desire for control. That may also indicate unhealthy soul ties. If you demand that family members always relate to you in an intimate or special way, and you experience emotional pain if they do not, you may need to be delivered from a soul tie.

> *If you demand that family members always relate to you in an intimate and special way, and you experience emotional pain if they do not, you may need to be delivered from a soul tie.*

For much of my adult life, I did not realize that I was bound by unhealthy soul ties to members of my family. I was unaware that I drew a sense of security and affirmation from family relationships that were extremely important to me—too important. If they did not meet my perceived need of their approbation and comfort, and a keen sense of belonging, I would experience emotional pain. The Holy Spirit showed me that my real problem was an unhealthy emotional dependency on people. But as I allowed Him to renew my mind, He began to heal my emotional wound. Then I began to look to God for His approval.

How often do we look to family or friends, even spouses, for the emotional security and affirmation that God gives us in relationship with Him alone? When family members do not live up to our expectations and we suffer in the misery of unforgiveness—that is an unhealthy soul tie. When we demand that they act in a certain way that is impossible or undesirable to them, we have an unhealthy soul tie to that person. In short, we have no right to dictate how others meet our emotional needs.

I have known young people who have felt trapped by their parents' desires for them. They did not feel free to choose a career or a spouse for themselves. These unhappy youth could not make adult decisions based on their own desires. These decisions were made for them by their parents who had decided what was best for them. Often, this domineering attitude causes the sons and daughters to become resentful and bitter toward their parents. They feel that they are not free to be the person who they really are. When parents try to live out their own goals for their children, this, too, demonstrates an unhealthy control over their lives—or a soul tie.

These are just a few examples of soul ties that occur within families. In a healthy family, each member will respect the other without trying to control them. Demanding that emotional needs be met is often a sign of an unhealthy soul tie that can have devastating consequences. The nature of divine love is to free the loved one of the tie, so that they can pursue life and their destiny in God.

Soul Ties in Friendships

If you asked Justine to describe her emotional life, she would tell you, "I was born half-sad. I don't ever remember feeling a sense of belonging or of being at peace with myself." She was not aware that being "half-sad" was not the will of God for His children. As I have explained, Jesus said He came that we might have abundant life. (See John 10:10.) Abundant life is not a half-sad life. Then why is it that so many Christians can relate to Justine's description of emotional sadness? I believe it is because they do not understand this journey to wholeness, the ongoing work of the Holy Spirit to renew their minds and heal their emotions.

Justine did not understand why she repeatedly ended up in exclusive relationships. She only knew that she only felt emotionally secure in relationships where she had the other person's total devotion. Only in feeling like she belonged to a person did she find relief from the painful emptiness she felt in her psyche and emotions. Justine did not know that God wanted to fill her emptiness with His love, joy, and peace. Instead, she suffered the pangs of emotional soul ties that bound her, first to one person and then another.

If you do not feel free to be your own person in a friendship, serving God and others, beware of spiritual bondage. An inordinate loyalty that keeps you in an exclusive relationship, limiting your activities and pursuit of other godly relationships, is symptomatic of a soul tie that can destroy your life.

> *If you do not feel free to be your own person in a friendship, serving God and others, beware of spiritual bondage.*

Even in marriage, where exclusivity is a normal element of a healthy relationship, a spouse can become overly possessive if he or she has an unhealthy soul tie. The deep friendship that characterizes a healthy marriage must not become so paramount that a spouse feels that he or she cannot develop other godly friendships. A relationship that is exclusive is sometimes threatened by careers, activities, service, and/or other godly friendships.

These codependent relationships are characterized by onerous possessiveness. They become a substitute for the healthy dependence we should have in our relationship with God. God alone is the source of our security and our emotional and mental well-being. As we allow the Holy Spirit to restore our souls to the wholeness Jesus offered, we will experience freedom in all our family and friend relationships.

Soul Ties of Sexual Immorality

According to the Scriptures, illicit sexual relationships outside of marriage create unhealthy soul ties. These sexual relations have a powerful impact on your psyche. The apostle Paul condemned sexual relationships outside of marriage:

> *Know ye not that your bodies are the members of Christ? Shall I then take the members of Christ, and make them the members of an harlot? God forbid. What? Know ye not that he which is joined to an harlot is one body? For two, saith [Jesus], shall be one flesh....Flee fornication.*
> (1 Corinthians 6:15–16, 18)

The reality of unhealthy soul ties created from becoming *"one flesh"* with another has been entirely overlooked by a generation that has embraced one-night stands as a part of the dating process. But that does not change the negative impact of illicit sexual relationships outside of marriage. Jesus explained the reality of becoming *"one flesh"*:

> *For this reason a man shall leave his father and mother and be joined to his wife, and the two shall become one flesh...So then, they are no longer two but one flesh.*
> (Matthew 19:5–6 NKJV)

In marriage, it is a beautiful experience to become *"one flesh"* with your spouse, as God intended. Apart from marriage, that act of intimacy creates painful soul ties that unwittingly bind you emotionally and psychologically to your sexual partner. That is why you suffer emotional pangs, even after the relationship has ended. You still desire the approval, affirmation, and even the intimacy you experienced in becoming one flesh with that partner.

I have ministered spiritual healing to people who have had so many sexual partners that they can't remember all their names. Most often, these experiences have happened before they were born again; yet there is still evidence of deep mental wounds from the soul ties that these illicit relationships created. Sometimes the person is tormented by recurring dreams or painful memories; some suffer inordinate longings for the partner. And they condemn themselves for still desiring one of their partners, thinking, *If only to talk with them.*

The good news is that I have witnessed the freedom these sincere believers enjoy when they pray to be released from the soul ties created by sexual sin. As they renounced each illicit relationship (all that they could remember) and broke its influence over their minds, they asked God to forgive and cleanse their soul. And they forgave their partner(s), as well. Many have shared testimonies of the joy and freedom they have experienced after being released from their torment. Their radiant faces attest to the freedom and wholeness they have received, as the Holy Spirit healed them of their hidden wounds.

To renounce soul ties in any inordinate or sinful relationship allows the light of God to dispel the darkness of our souls. It releases the blood of Jesus to cleanse our hearts and heal us from the spiritual bondage of unhealthy soul ties. Along with forgiving those who have harmed us, our own choice to turn away from darkness to His wonderful light brings healing and the closure that we so desperately need. As we continue our journey into freedom through our sanctification, we will discover more and more the fullness of God's love.

> *To renounce soul ties in any inordinate or sinful relationship allows the light of God to dispel the darkness of our souls.*

THE FULLNESS OF
GOD'S LOVE—PART I[21]

G od the Father, God the Son, and God the Holy Spirit—the triune Godhead—are one God. And the Scriptures declare that *"God is love"* (1 John 4:8). We cannot humanly comprehend the essence of this divine Trinity, which dwells in the mystery of perfect love and harmony as one God. Yet we learn from the Scriptures certain biblical expressions of divine love that corresponds to each Person of the Godhead: the Father, the Son, and the Holy Spirit.

For example, the Scriptures teach that the Holy Spirit has come as our Comforter, Teacher, and Guide into all truth. One of His divine tasks is to reveal Jesus to our hearts. (See John 16:13–15.) And Jesus came to reveal the Father. He told His disciples, *"He that hath seen me hath seen the Father"* (John 14:9). The Scriptures also teach that the Father sent the Son to become our Savior. (See John 3:16.) The heavenly Father declared on

21. The concept of comparing the father figure to God, siblings to Jesus, and the mother figure to the Holy Spirit in chapters 8 and 9 are taken from Dawna De Silva and Teresa Liebscher, *Sozo Basic Training Manual* (2011).

more than one occasion, *"This is my beloved Son, in whom I am well pleased"* (Matthew 3:17).

Recognizing the different qualities of the Persons of the Godhead can help us to properly relate to them. As God's born-again children, we can receive the love and affirmation we need from our heavenly Father; we can open our hearts to receive the Holy Spirit, our divine Comforter; and we can relate intimately to Christ, our Savior, who is our elder Brother and Friend, as well.

However, we may be hindered in receiving the wonderful love of God in all its expression if we have been wounded by some of the most important human relationships. For example, if our relationship with our earthly father was unhealthy, we may view our heavenly Father through distorted lenses.

Recognizing Your Wounds

As I learned in assessing my childhood trauma, it is difficult to determine the powerful impact that our wounds play in shaping our reactions to everyday occurrences. Often, we simply perceive our painful reactions to life as normal and expect others to react as we do in similar life situations. We do not realize that our strong negative reactions in adult relationships and even in our relationship with God may be rooted in the wounds of our past.

For many years, I was skeptical about the emphasis some valid streams of ministry put upon understanding your "inner child." I feared that these sincere spiritual leaders were using a psychological approach to remedy spiritual problems. And I believed that born-again Christians needed only to believe that they were "new creatures in Christ Jesus" and that as old things passed away, all things became new. (See 2 Corinthians 5:17.)

I also embraced the apostle Paul's admonition of *"forgetting those things which are behind, and reaching forth unto those things which are before"* (Philippians 3:13). A closer look at the context of Paul's statement, however, shows that he was *"forgetting"* his wonderful pedigree as a Jew among Jews. He was leaving behind his own righteousness based on the law and not on *"the righteousness which is of God by faith"* (Philippians 3:9). And, as I have mentioned, Paul wrote much about the necessary sanctification process of our soul, which involves letting go of the things of the past.

> *The sanctification process of our soul involves letting go of the things of the past.*

A careful reading of the apostle Paul's letters to the churches reveals his emphasis on our relationship with God as the only source of the complete transformation of our soul: the way we *think*, our *emotional* well-being, and the decisions and choices of our *wills*. Paul exhorted believers to *"put off"* (Colossians 3:8) wrong emotional responses of the soul, which he refers to as the *"old man"* (verse 9). And he continually exhorted men to *"put on the new man, which is renewed in knowledge after the image of him that created him"* (verse 10).

As we recognize the faulty thinking and wounded emotional responses of our psyche, we *will* be transformed by the renewing of our mind. As we choose to repent and then to forgive those who may be responsible for our pain, we will enter into greater dimensions of the *"righteousness, and peace, and joy in the Holy Ghost"* (Romans 14:17).

I now realize that until the Holy Spirit began to reveal to me my need for putting off my unhealthy emotional responses to my friends, I was not really free in these areas of my soul. For example, the peace and joy Jesus promised me were continually threatened in any situation of life that I perceived to be, even remotely, another abandonment. I needed the sanctifying work of the Holy Spirit to renew my mind so that I felt secure in God's love, regardless of the ever-changing relationships in my life.

Our tendency to transfer our faulty perception of earthly relationships to our relationship with God is somewhat valid. It has helped many believers renounce the lies they believe about God and to receive His great love for them, for a man whose earthly father is loving and affirming may picture his heavenly Father in that same way. On the other hand, a man whose earthly father is seemed aloof or absent to him as a boy may picture his heavenly Father very unlike the former.

It is sad that we can live our whole lives with a wounded soul, not understanding what the abundant life that Jesus has promised really looks like— all because we have not understood the dynamic work of the Holy Spirit to renew our minds and heal our minds of the wounds of our past.

The Dissolution of the Family Unit

Family relationships perhaps have the greatest influence on our emotional and mental health. From birth, we are totally dependent on our fathers and mothers to meet our basic needs for survival. Siblings, too, can positively or negatively influence our young lives.

> *Family relationships have the greatest influence on our emotional and mental health.*

A general consensus in our nation of the growing malaise and dissolution of the family unit is that it is having disastrous effects on the health of our "national psyche." Statistics show an alarming rise of divorce cases, children born to single mothers, and children who are abused by their parents or siblings. Children of absent or disengaged fathers develop faulty perceptions of what a father is and develop emotional voids and deep insecurities. We must take a moment to consider the faultiness behind what this generation considers to be normal relationships, both with family members and significant others, as well as with authority figures.

Unfortunately, the church has not been exempt from the alarming family breakdowns in our nation. The number of divorce cases of those in the church are not significantly different from those who do not attend church. The same professional and material demands that affect nonbelievers affect Christians; and the stress of these pursuits is only compounded when our basic needs of belonging and emotional security go unmet.

It is interesting to note that one ethnic group is largely immune to this national disintegration of the family unit: the Jewish family. Data shows much lower statistics of divorce and single parent families within the Jewish community. A study in 2009 shows that 72 percent of Orthodox Jewish men and 74 percent of Jewish women rate their marriage as excellent or very good, while according to General Social Survey of 2009, only 63 percent of men and 60 percent of women who were non-Jews in the US rated their marriage excellent or very good.[22] And there is a very small percentage of Jewish males who are imprisoned, as compared to other ethnic groups.

22. http://www.ou.org/ou/print_this/64625

Researchers believe that the biblically based approach for rearing children in the Jewish community is largely responsible for these strikingly different results. For example, Jewish families typically consist of a strong and engaged father who pronounces a patriarchal blessing over his children often. He spends quality time with them and also imparts to them the family values and wisdom on how to organize their priorities. These values include a sense of loyalty to their family members and a sense of pride in them, as well. This sense of belonging to family and the larger Jewish community builds a strong accountability system for the children and fosters a secure environment in which they can develop their sense of worth and learn their purpose in life.

God's plan for the instruction and blessing of children by committed parents is designed to develop in them a healthy mind. As our society turns from these godly principles for family and adopts a hedonistic, self-serving lifestyle, the psychological health of our nation will continue to decline. The devastating results of this decline are apparent in our youth and family units today. The rise of illicit drug use, alcohol consumption, domestic violence, and the need for government programs to protect our children all are stark evidence of the breakdown of the family unit in our nation.

Who Is a Father?

I shared earlier that a key component of my personal emotional healing was learning my true identity as a born-again child of God. Discovering my heavenly Father's love for me and His destiny for my life has been a liberating therapy for my soul.

Yet merely understanding that God is a loving heavenly Father does not liberate us. As a pastor, I have learned that when explaining to a new believer that God is a loving heavenly father, I may receive differing responses. It is natural for them to associate the term *father* with the person in their lives whom they called "father" as a child. If this earthly relationship was not a strong, loving one, they may have difficulty picturing a loving heavenly Father who cares deeply for them. On the other hand, it is even more difficult for those who were deprived of a father growing up difficult.

There is no way to circumvent the effects of your history if you have suffered a painful relationship with your earthly father. Many children have suffered the neglect of an absent father; others have never even met their fathers;

still others have lived their lives trying to please an overly strict father who made them feel that they could never measure up. In short, we all have developed faulty impressions of who our heavenly Father is based on our personal experience with the man we call "Dad."

> *We have all developed faulty impressions of who our heavenly Father is based on our personal experience with the man we call "Dad."*

The Absent Father

As a boy, George saw very little of his father. He came to understand early in life that he had to look to his mother for whatever he needed. When his father was around, he was pleasant enough and sometimes brought him little gifts. Once, he gave him a shiny pocketknife and on another occasion, a cool slingshot. Occasionally, his dad would bring him a leftover pastry or two from the bakery where he worked. But apart from these scant memories, there just didn't seem to be any real connection to or interaction with this man he called Dad.

As an adult, George tried to remember if his father ever told him stories or played games with him, took him places or just spent time with him. He couldn't. Nor could he remember simple pleasant conversations with his dad, such as, "I love you, Son," or "How was your day at school?" George didn't have a grandfather or uncle who could fill the role of a loving father figure. So he simply embraced the reality of his absent father: *This is what fathers are like.*

It is a well-known fact that fathers are the parents who most help children develop a healthy identity of themselves. The father has the innate ability to make his children feel secure in their identity. An absent father predisposes the child to identity struggles, which lead to painful insecurities. This lack of loving interaction between the father and the child also causes the child to question his or her personal value and worth. Many of these children lack a sense of purpose and wonder why in the world they are here.

Since George never had a loving, nurturing relationship with his father, he did not have a healthy picture of what a father/son relationship should look like. He gave His heart to Jesus as a child and began to seek God, desiring to really know Him. Yet he could not seem to grasp the reality of his heavenly Father's love for him. He still struggled to understand his personal worth, destiny, and purpose in life.

For example, when George prayed, He would address Jesus, but he would never pray to his heavenly Father. The fact is that he could not trust his heavenly Father to be there for him anymore than his earthly father had been. Because this profound relational wound between his earthly father and himself had not been healed, George continued to struggle to understand his personal identity. He lived his life trying to prove his own self worth and to convince himself he was a valuable person.

George's peers admired him as a person of many accomplishments. His children were blessed with a father who was always there for them, a father who met every need. George had determined to fix his life—to prove his worth—through personal achievement that would make him "somebody." In doting on his children and providing for their every whim, he was unconsciously trying to fill his yawning chasm of emptiness. He was compensating for the silent cry of his childhood: *Does my daddy know I'm here?*

Though by the world's standards, George would be considered a successful man—he was dearly loved by his own family—he was still driven to overachieving. He struggled with the need to continually establish his identity through good works and recognition among his peers. He has not yet discovered the truth that what his earthly father was not, his heavenly Father could be for him—an ever-present Father who would always be there.

Until George receives this revelation, he will always be searching for his identity by overachieving and meeting others' needs. In that way, he expects to compensate for his own insecurities and lack of purpose. He will continue to suffer from the feeling that he can never be good enough, because he does not know himself as a beloved son of God.

George needs to know that his heavenly Father has sent both Jesus and the Holy Spirit to live in his heart for the purpose of bringing him close to Himself. This wonderful revelation of the loving heavenly Father is all that can heal George's wounded heart. How God the Father must long to deliver George from the agony of that same little boy, who still longs for the affirmation of his father.

The Impossible-to-Please Father

Jenifer's friends were mystified that this woman who was so talented and beautiful could appear so insecure regarding her personal identity and sense of worth. Like George, Jenifer continually sought for recognition in life situations; she referred to her desperate search for identity as "needing to find her place."

Even after she became a born-again believer, Jenifer did not feel secure in her position in life. Did God love her as much as He loved others? Had He overlooked her abilities? Jenifer's real problem was not her lack of position in life; rather, it was the lack of understanding her proper identity, which had stemmed from her childhood relationship with her father.

As a young child, Jenifer learned that the only way she could hope to be noticed by her father was to excel in what she did, in achieving top honors for her efforts. She understood intuitively that his approval came only by *doing* something that he considered exceptional. He never applauded her for simply *being* his daughter.

Most of the time, Jenifer never felt that she measured up to his idea of a perfect daughter, no matter how well she did in school or other pursuits. As a result, her adult mind embraced the idea that her personal identity and worth were based solely on her ability to excel—to do the best and be the best among her peers.

Jenifer unconsciously associated her ability to do the best with being loved and appreciated. People who were most loved and appreciated were those who filled the most important positions or completed the most important assignments. As a result, if she perceived that her position was lesser than that of her peers, her sense of worth took a direct hit; she felt her identity was negated.

To some observers, Jenifer's painful struggle with a lack of self-worth may have looked like an ego trip. However, that could not be further from the truth. The root of Jenifer's identity crisis was actually an unhealed emotional wound inflicted by her aloof, impossible-to-please father.

For Jenifer, the concept of *father* was a person who was disinterested, disengaged, aloof, and hard to satisfy. He did not affirm his daughter for the beautiful person she was; he was only impressed when she took the title of top honors for what she *did*. Naturally, she evaluated her sense of worth in her mind based on how important her job was and how well she did her job.

Jenifer desperately needed a loving relationship with her heavenly Father. She needed to experience the supernatural love of His heart that adored her for who He made her to be—not for what she could *do* for Him. And she needed to understand the impartial love of God for all His children. The apostle Peter declared, *"I perceive that God is no respecter of persons"* (Acts 10:34). And so He is no respecter of persons. Only He could heal her wounded mind and exchange her faulty perception of her self-worth with the identity of a daughter of Christ—the high value He places on all His children.

Healing for the Father Wound

Happily, after Jenifer was born again, she began to read the Scriptures avidly, several hours every day. As she pored over the promises of God, she began to discover her heavenly Father's love for her. Slowly, the light of God dawned in her soul, and she realized that she had believed a lie: God could not be trusted with her emotional needs. She realized that she could present to Him her legitimate needs of affirmation and self-worth. The Holy Spirit revealed to her that God loved her for who she *was*, not for what she *did*. Jenifer read the words of Jesus that described her heavenly Father's love in an incredible way:

> *Are not two sparrows sold for a farthing? And one of them shall not fall on the ground without your Father. But the very hairs of your head are all numbered. Fear ye not therefore, ye are of more value than many sparrows.* (Matthew 10:29–31)

Jenifer's response to such wonderful, attentive care from her heavenly Father was at first incredulous. She thought to herself, *My heavenly Father numbers the hairs of my head? Really? I know His Word is true. That has been proved by the joy and peace I have found in His salvation. So I must have been deceived. My heavenly Father values me more than I can imagine; His attention to every insignificant sparrow proves that. How could He be so tender? So caring? I love Him for loving the sparrows. And He tells me not to be afraid. I was afraid to trust Him, because I believed Satan's lie that He would treat me like my earthly father did.*

She wept at the revelation of such a loving Father's heart. The more she embraced the truth that God loved her as her earthly father had not, the greater healing she experienced of the father wound.

The turning point for Jenifer was when she chose to trust God and take Him at His Word. She began to pray for the strength to forgive her earthly father who had failed to love her as she needed him to. As she did, she felt God's love for her fill her heart. And, surprisingly, she began to feel His love for her father, as well.

Just as the devil raised suspicion in Adam and Eve's heart about God's love for them when he tempted them to disobey His commands, so he tries to do the same to born-again believers. However unconscious it is, when we try to relate to God as we relate to imperfect human relationships, we will inevitably live in fear and unbelief.

Jenifer also discovered that her heavenly Father delights to give good things to those who ask. (See Matthew 7:11.) She began to accept the truth that as His child, He would be happy to give good things to her. Then she heard Him say, "I give good things to them that *ask.*" Startled, she thought, *I haven't trusted Him enough to ask Him. I'm just going to start asking.* And so in response to Jenifer's requests, her faithful heavenly Father began to release divine gifts and abilities into her life, which empowered her to fulfill her divine destiny. He filled her with compassion for other hurting people.

Jenifer takes pleasure in sharing with others the keys she has learned to walk in the freedom of abundant life. She understands how the enemy of our souls is tormenting them. Patiently, and step-by-step, she leads these precious believers into an understanding of their loving heavenly Father, just as she discovered Him for herself. She shares with them the character of God revealed in the Scriptures and the personal value He places on His sons and daughters. She helps them to renounce the lies that the enemy has used to deceive them and to use the key of forgiveness to open their prison doors.

Likewise, when we, as believers, experience the liberating power of *sozo*, we are set free and equipped to do the work of the ministry. As we yield to the ongoing sanctifying work of the Holy Spirit in our lives, we are empowered to share the gospel of wholeness, just as Jenifer is doing.

> *When we, as believers, experience the liberating power of sozo, we are set free and equipped to do the work of the ministry.*

While people may judge you as prideful, angry, self-absorbed, insecure, selfish, or fearful, Jesus simply sees you as a person who needs to be saved from destructive wounds. Whether these wounds are caused by your sin or the sin of others committed against you, Jesus came to set you free. To Him, you are simply a lost soul bound in your unhealed state and in desperate need of a Savior. And He died to offer you the wholeness that only God's love can give.

Your Father Figure

Your father figure may fit the paradigm of an absent dad or a hard-to-please dad or an I-never-knew-him dad. Even if you have a wonderful father, he still fits into the category of a less-than-perfect father. Whatever your experience is with Dad, you can expect it to affect your perception of your heavenly Father.

It is as we allow the Holy Spirit to shine His light in our hearts that we recognize the awesome truth of our heavenly Father's love for us. Like Jenifer, when we begin, even tentatively, to receive that wonderful truth, we will be set free to experience His love. And as we pursue Him, asking for the love that we need, He has promised to give it to us. Jesus declared that if we continue in the Word, we will know the truth, and the truth will set us free. (See John 8:31–32.)

It is the work of the Holy Spirit to renew your mind with His truth; it is your part to allow Him to do so. As your mind is renewed with the truth of God, you will embrace your great worth and your true identity as part of the family of God. When you choose to forgive your earthly father's failures, the Holy Spirit will empower you to walk in the freedom of your heavenly Father's great love. It is then that you will be able to fulfill the destiny God ordained for you.

A healthy mind will be yours if you embrace this divine love relationship with your heavenly Father. When you are reconciled to Christ by placing your faith in Him, God your heavenly Father becomes your Protector, Friend, Companion, and the always-there-for-you Guide. He fills you with the security of divine purpose, for which you were created. He reveals to you His divine destiny for your life, which will establish your true identity for all of time and eternity. You will never again have to wonder who you are or why you are here. Even Old Testament saints understood the divine reality of this great, loving heart of the Father:

> *A father of the fatherless, and a judge of the widows, is God in his holy habitation.* (Psalm 68:5)

> *Like as a father pitieth his children, so the Lord pitieth them that fear him.* (Psalm 103:13)

On this earth, we will never be able to comprehend the profound intimacy shared between Jesus and God the Father. Consider the insight Christ gives to us as He appealed to His heavenly Father just before He was crucified:

> *Father, the hour is come; glorify thy Son, that thy Son also may glorify thee...And now I am no more in the world, but these [men] are in the world, and I come to thee. Holy Father, keep through thine own name those whom thou hast given me, that they may be one, as we are.... Sanctify them through thy truth: thy word is truth....Neither pray I for these alone, but for them also which shall believe on me through their word; that they all may be one; **as thou, Father, art in me, and I in thee, that they also may be one in us**: that the world may believe that thou has sent me.* (John 17:1, 11, 17, 20–21)

Have you begun to grasp the intimacy shared between the heavenly Father and His only begotten Son, which Jesus reveals to us in this poignant prayer? And do you hear the yearning cry of Jesus for you to share in that divine intimacy with them? Jesus came to restore unto His Father a family who will love Him eternally and of which every born-again believer is an integral member.

When you walk in the freedom of your identity as a child of God and learn to walk in His divine destiny, you will discover the only life that will ever satisfy your heart. It is to be in relationship with your heavenly Father that you were created. And your heavenly Father has promised never to leave you or forsake you. (See Hebrews 13:5.)

> *It is to be in relationship with your heavenly Father that you were created.*

As I mentioned, there are aspects of your relationship with God that resemble your relationship with other members of your family. For example, the role of mother is often to comfort and to teach. In that sense, your relationship with her resembles God's expression of love through the Holy Spirit who is named our Comforter and our Guide.

And the role of siblings your life is to be companions, encouragers, and friends, who relate to the same father and mother. In that sense, Jesus called His disciples not servants but friends, because He had told them everything He had heard from Father. (See John 15:15.) In the next chapter, we will examine how these other familial relationships—with your mother and your siblings (or lack of them)—can affect your relationship with Jesus and the Holy Spirit.

THE FULLNESS OF
GOD'S LOVE—PART II

I n the last chapter, I gave a brief description of the mystery of the triune Godhead, functioning in total harmony as the Father, the Son, and the Holy Spirit. As the essence of love, God expresses His divine nature in different ways. We have considered the love of our heavenly Father and the ways in which our earthly fathers impact our perception of Him. In this chapter, we will consider briefly how our earthly relationships with our mothers and our sibling(s) impact our perception of God the Holy Spirit and God the Son, respectively.

What Is a Mother?

Generally speaking, earthly mothers are primarily the parent who comforts the crying infant, bandages the child's wounds, and listens to the teen's daily "tragedies." Unfortunately, some mothers are simply not there for their children. They involve themselves in pursuits of personal goals and aspirations, and neglect to care for their children. Sadly, others are simply not there, because they are forced to work long hours outside of the home to provide for their family. Still others may have been taken prematurely from their families by disease or accident.

On the other hand, there are mothers who are there for their children. But instead of offering the nurture and comfort their children need, they set such high standards for them that are impossible to reach. These children live with the constant disapproval of their demanding mothers and grow discouraged from even trying.

Still other mothers, perhaps reacting out of their own wounds, speak harshly to their children; they never seem to have a soft lap where their children can cuddle and hear kind affirmation.

Whatever the mother scenario, when children have not experienced a mother's loving nurture and comfort, they don't realize that there is comfort for their hurts. They may try to fill that void with a myriad of substitutes that make them feel good.

It is wonderful to know that God, the Holy Spirit, has been sent by our Lord Jesus to be our divine Comforter. He lives in the spirits of born-again believers. Jesus promised His disciples, *"I will pray the Father, and he shall give you another Comforter, that he may abide with you for ever, even the Spirit of truth"* (John 14:16–17). Having the presence of God dwell within us and allowing Him to speak to us and lead us securely through life removes all fear and stress from our earthly journey.

If you have suffered a lack of comfort or nurture from your earthly mother, you may have a wounded mind that hinders you from receiving the Holy Spirit's divine comfort. You may suffer the pangs of insecurity and stress, not knowing that you can approach God for comfort. Many look to illicit relationships or destructive habits (drug addiction, alcohol) to find temporary comfort, or at least to escape the pain and stress created from their mother wound.

If you have suffered a lack of comfort of nurture from your earthly mother, you may have a wounded mind that hinders you from receiving the Holy Spirit's divine comfort.

As adults, people who did not have a nurturing mother often have difficulty relating to the Holy Spirit, who dwells in their spirit and has an interest in their daily concerns. They have a hard time believing that He is aware of their desires and wants to guide their every decision. Have you ever heard people say that they don't want to "bother God" with their insignificant little need? These people are survivors. They learned not to cry when they scrape their knee, because there is no one to hear.

If a mother has been impossible to please, her adult child(ren) may view the comfort of the Holy Spirit as unattainable to them. They may think that God is surely more impossible to please than their mother. Instead of seeking God for divine comfort, they cringe in fear that they might displease Him with their requests.

Dr. Gabor Mate identifies three great stressors that threaten our physical and psychological survival. They are…

1. Uncertainty

2. Lack of needed information

3. Loss of control

In our complex, fast-moving world, no one is exempt from these stressors and their effects. Rich and poor alike are vulnerable to the uncertainty of the present and the future. Even with Facebook and Twitter, along with other social media networks, we still lack the information we need to resolve life's issues. And no one can control the unforeseen circumstances, relationship difficulties, and tragedies that come our way.

As children, we naturally look to our mothers to teach us, inform us, and help us handle the stress of known and unknown situations. As adults, we must learn to turn to God, who alone supplies us with the information, the wisdom, and divine revelation we need to live a confident and peaceful life.

Learning to yield our lives to the Holy Spirit daily and to hear His voice provides us with greater security than the best portfolio or any other natural source of earthly security. We don't need to fear losing our way in life when we faithfully follow our divine Guide; He will convict us of sin and lead us into all truth. (See John 16:8, 13.) And He will also comfort our hearts with the promises of God's Word, as He reveals Jesus Himself in our hearts. This is a much different mind-set than a worldly mind-set, which is threatened by a future of uncertainty, war, chaos, and loss of control. In order to enjoy the benefits of God's kingdom—the righteousness, peace, and joy of the Holy Spirit (see Romans 14:17)—we need the Holy Spirit to heal our hearts and reveal Jesus to us.

> *In order to enjoy the benefits of God's kingdom, we need the Holy Spirit to heal our hearts and reveal Jesus to us.*

In the book of Acts, we see a wonderful testimony of the early Christians, who were bathed in the presence of the Holy Spirit:

> *Then had the churches **rest** throughout all Judaea and Galilee and Samaria, and were edified; and walking in the fear of the Lord, and in the comfort of the Holy Ghost, were multiplied.* (Acts 9:31)

These early Christians entered a time of rest, prosperity, and peace as they walked in the comfort of the Holy Spirit. Not only were they personally edified—built up in their spiritual strength—but their number was multiplied, as well. They were experiencing the ministry of the Holy Spirit that brought health to their souls. He gave them rest from their enemies, and many people were drawn to the Lord. Their enemies undoubtedly witnessed the peace and joy of God in their lives.

If you recognize in yourself a reluctance or inability to seek comfort in the presence of the Holy Spirit, you may be suffering from a mother wound. I encourage you to ask the Holy Spirit to show you why you cannot receive His divine comfort, and then to forgive your mother for her failing you as a child in whatever way. As you forgive her and believe that God is your true source of comfort, He will be faithful to heal your wound and set you free.

As you forgive your mother and believe that God is your true source of comfort, He will be faithful to heal your wound and set you free.

The Companionship of a Brother, Sister, and Friend

Our earthly siblings can become our best friends or our bitter rivals. Some siblings may simply become disinterested and distance themselves from us; the most they have in common with us is sharing the same childhood, parents, and home. They can even become enemies for life, displaying jealousy or contempt for our abilities or some other aspect of our character. Or they may involuntarily abandon us through an untimely death, breaking our hearts. For some who have not grown up with siblings, lack of family bonding can result in a sense of loneliness or an inability to relate to people as close friends and companions.

In a similar manner, as we develop close friendships, we risk being hurt and offended, just as siblings can do to one another. As fallen people in a fallen world, siblings and friends may disappoint us in many ways. In short, our life experiences with (or without) siblings and friends can negatively impact our mental health. And they can hinder our perception of Jesus, who wants to relate to us as an elder Brother, divine Companion, and Friend.

While the Scriptures teach that Jesus is our Savior, they also declare that Jesus is not ashamed to call us His brethren. (See Hebrews 2:11–12.) And Jesus told His disciples that they were His friends, because He had shared all things with them. (See John 15:15.) It is difficult to imagine walking with God in an intimacy similar to what we share with our loyal and trusted friends. Yet He initiated that idea and desires to commune with us—Friend to friend.

What happens, then, if we impose our earthly perceptions of sibling and friend relationships on our relationship with Him? The biblical description of how Jesus envisions a relationship with us is as two equals, coming together. This idea may be distorted in our minds if we have been wounded by a brother, sister, or friend. As a result of our painful experience, which needs to be healed, we may find it difficult to trust Jesus with our deepest affection.

Jesus personally understood the pain that can be inflicted by brothers and sisters. His brothers were, shall we say, less than understanding of their elder brother who taught the multitudes and worked all kinds of miracles. On one occasion, they taunted Jesus, saying He should show His miracles to the world. The Scriptures record their rejection of Jesus: *"For neither did his brethren believe in him"* (John 7:5).

The Scriptures also record times when Jesus' followers—or friends—left Him because of His teaching. (See John 6:66.) And His disciples continually misunderstood Him. Peter denied Him, and Judas betrayed Him.

Jesus experienced the emotional pain from these unfaithful siblings and friends. Yet He showed us how to live above sin, forgiving and loving those who sinned against us. He patiently taught His disciples what they needed to know about His kingdom, though they did not understand. And He prayed for His friends, as He did for Peter, reinstating him as His disciple after His resurrection.

When we have brothers or sisters who do not support our goals and dreams and fail to be a friend to us, it is natural be hurt, offended, and disappointed. Their unloving responses leave us feeling devalued or ignored, which can cause deep wounds in our mind. This painful abandonment is another reason why we truly need to discover the Savior and Friend who will walk with us faithfully and impart to us His life and love continually.

Jesus expressed His desire for this intimate relationship with His friends when He prayed that His Father would allow us to be one with the Trinity, to be in Them and They in us. (See John 17:11–26.) Those believers who see Jesus simply as their Savior and the Giver of eternal life, as wonderful as that is, are being deprived of a deeper, more intimate communion with Him, the perfect Brother and Friend.

Believers who see Jesus simply as their Savior are being deprived of a deeper, more intimate communion with Him, the perfect Brother and Friend.

Many people have experienced wonderful relationships with their brothers and sisters, who are deeply trusted friends. Then, tragically, they are taken away by disease or accident, suffering an untimely death. The pain of losing that dear relationship can wound the mind in such a way that the person does not want to get close to another person so as not to suffer such a devastating loss again.

Robert Murray McCheyne, a notable pastor and revivalist who lived during the 1800's, suffered the loss of a dear brother when he was in his teens. McCheyne felt that he could not live without his brother. In his agony, he wrote with great sadness, "I...began to seek a brother who cannot die."

Jesus Christ, our lovely Savior, has become that Brother to all who believe on His name. He wants to heal the wounds from all hurtful relationships and become to us the perfect Brother and Friend, who will always be there for us. He will support and sustain us, believe in us, and transform us into His image, granting us freedom to fulfill the destiny He has ordained for us.

Redefining Friendship

In our generation, we are witnessing a phenomenon of increasing avenues of communication, chatting with Facebook friends, texting, tweeting, and whatever comes next. Is it possible that we are redefining the fundamental meaning of friendship? Without discounting the merits of friendly communication by whatever means, we must be careful not to equate shallow conversations about mundane details of life, unsolicited opinions from newsfeeds, and other irrelevant information with the biblical concept of friendship.

These communication outlets are not viable substitutes for deep friendship—committing to godly brothers and sisters—which involves transparency, counsel, and deep affection for one another. These are people who share our dreams and vision for divine destiny, who pray for us and celebrate our victories in God. Being a vital member of the body of Christ by engaging in these relationships is key to walking in the freedom of wholeness in God.

> *Being a vital member of the body of Christ and engaging in transparent relationships with other believers is key to walking the in the freedom of wholeness in God.*

During those painful months I suffered from debilitating sickness, I was very grateful for friends who came to my house and prayed with me every day. They never allowed weariness or busyness to deter them. One day, a friend brought me a worship CD with gentle, inspiring music, along with a scented candle. It was her way of saying, "I'm sorry for your pain. Let me try to make it a little better."

Another friend actually brought a newborn baby lamb into my house for me to see and to hold. She just wanted to remind me of the gentle Lamb of God who loves me. These kind gestures became tiny portraits of the tender love of Jesus, who is present when we need Him, full of compassion and uplifting to our soul.

Putting an End to the Lies

To experience *sozo*, complete wholeness for your soul, you need to be aware of God's divine love that He offers to His children. As your heavenly Father—your Comforter and Guide, your elder Brother and Friend—the triune Godhead wants to invade your mind and bring healing to every wound. As I have mentioned, the iniquity of mankind permeates our lost soul in our sinful state. And the sin of other fallen people in our lives exacerbates our unhealed condition.

It bears repeating that Jesus came to destroy the works of the Evil One (see 1 John 3:8) and to set the captives free (see Luke 4:18). We simply need to recognize our desperate need for wholeness and cry out to God in faith that He will set us free. We need to renounce the lies that enter our minds through our sin and receive the truth of *sozo*—wholeness—for our soul.

The psalmist declared, "*As the deer pants for the water brooks, so pants my soul for You, O God. My soul thirsts for God, for the living God....Deep calls unto deep at the noise of Your waterfalls*" (Psalm 42:1–2, 7 NKJV). Your need for God is no less desperate than the deer's desperate need for water, which he cannot live without.

Your soul will not be healed (renewed or sanctified) if you settle for a superficial understanding of your wounds. You need to open your heart to receive the depths of healing that God—your loving heavenly Father, your Savior, elder Brother, Friend, and divine Comforter—offers to you freely.

God's plan for redemption is to preserve you blameless—spirit, soul, and body—until the coming of the Lord Jesus Christ. (See 1 Thessalonians 5:23.) To that end, Jesus promised to send to us the Comforter, the third Person of the triune Godhead, to lead us into all truth. (See John 16:7, 13.)

Do you believe your heavenly Father truly loves you and wants the best for you? Are you convinced that you can trust Jesus to always be there for you, first as your Savior, then as your elder Brother and Friend? Can you receive the comfort of the Holy Spirit in every painful situation in your life and yield to Him to guide you into all truth? Do you believe that God cares about every detail of your life?

If not, you can be set free by acknowledging the wounds of your soul. As you forgive family members and friends who have caused you to doubt the love of God, you will begin to enjoy the rest that Jesus has promised for those who come to Him:

> *Come unto me, all ye that labour and are heavy laden, and I will give you rest. Take my yoke upon you, and learn of me; for I am meek and lowly in heart: and ye shall find rest unto your souls. For my yoke is easy, and my burden is light.* (Matthew 11:28–30)

Jesus promised that if we abide by His Word, we will know the truth, and the truth will set us free. (See John 8:32.) Ask the Holy Spirit to lead you into truth, to show you the reality of Jesus' love, and to reveal to you the loving heart of your heavenly Father. When you do, He will be faithful to cleanse your mind of all lies and replace them with the truth of who God really is. When you begin to see Him as your Redeemer, Healer, Deliverer, best Friend, trusted Confidant, and divine Comforter, you will begin to *"prove what is that good, and acceptable, and perfect, will of God"* (Romans 12:2). That is kingdom living at its best!

10

CONQUERING
DIFFICULT WOUNDS

Why is it that certain painful symptoms in your mind, which you have faithfully renounced, continue to torment you, holding you in bondage? What makes complete freedom so illusive? Perhaps you have a measure of peace in your soul and confidence in your relationship with God. You rejoice in His goodness and in His renewing of your mind. You are so grateful that you have received His love.

Then, inexplicably, you find yourself reverting back to the muck and mire of those old tormenting thoughts and negative emotions. Continually plagued by these negative reactions, insecurities, and fears (from which you felt you were delivered), you become discouraged. You wonder, *Why can't I walk in that promised freedom that is clearly taught in the Scriptures?* Reader, hold on to Peter's promise:

> *But the God of all grace, who hath called us unto his eternal glory by Christ Jesus, after that ye have suffered a while, make you perfect, stablish, strengthen, settle you.* (1 Peter 5:10)

What a wonderful promise: we will be perfected, established, strengthened, and settled. Unfortunately, when old thinking patterns arise, along with negative emotional reactions, many believers lose heart and do not believe they can be truly freed from these ingrained mind-sets. They simply determine to love God and serve Him the best they can in order to receive their reward of eternal life in heaven. And they settle for lives marked by a certain hellishness of psychological pain they cannot seem to shake.

Jesus promised us that he will perfect us, establish us, strengthen us, and settle us.

Doors of Entry

In my book *Freer Than You Ever Dreamed*, I discussed in depth the understanding we received from Carlos Annacondia's ministry about the four doors of entry into our soul, which can bring us into bondage.[23] In his humble yet authoritative tone, Carlos Annacondia said to me, "You see, the devil cannot enter our lives without permission. But if we open a door to him, we are inviting his entrance." His words reminded me of the apostle Paul's exhortation to believers to give no place to the devil:

> *And be renewed in the spirit of your mind; and that ye put on the new man, which after God is created in righteousness and true holiness. Wherefore putting away lying, speak every man truth with his neighbour: for we are members one of another. Be ye angry, and sin not: let not the sun go down upon your wrath: **Neither give place to the devil**.*
>
> (Ephesians 4:23–27)

I began to contemplate what "giving place to the devil" meant for the sincere believer in Christ. According to the Scriptures, we can open a door to the enemy through sin and disobedience—essentially, our wrong choices.

---

23. The Argentinean pastor Pablo Bottari introduced the concept of four doors. See Appendix: The Four Doors.

For example, allowing anger and offense to remain in your heart opens a door to the enemy to disturb your peace as a believer.

On the other hand, a door may have been opened to the devil by trauma or rejection in your past, as we have discussed. An unhealed wound in your mind can still trigger negative thoughts and emotional reactions to day-to-day encounters. But the good news is that you can learn to recognize that door so that you can close it to the enemy.

As you seek God in prayer and in His Word, the Holy Spirit will be faithful to shine His light on any darkness within your soul. He will convict you and give you an opportunity to repent, closing the door to the devil's foothold in your mind as a believer. That is part of *put[ting] off the old man* (Colossians 3:9) and *put[ting] on the new man, which after God is created in righteousness and true holiness* (Ephesians 4:24).

The world uses cliché words and phrases, such as "having closure," that suggest you can put an end to the torment you have experienced, whether it is a painful loss or trauma or some other hardship. Perhaps these symbolic gestures help. But God's divine plan for your freedom from mental and emotional torment involves profound healing of your wounds. He closes the door to them and throws away the key.

> *God's divine plan for your freedom from mental and emotional torment involves profound healing of your wounds.*

Identifying the Doors

In their decades of ministering to hundreds of thousands of people, our Argentinian friends have narrowed the points of entry into our souls to four doors, which are...

1. Fear

2. Hatred

3. Sexual sin

4. Occult involvement

There is a list of sinful attitudes and practices that accompany each of these doors of access. For example, the door of fear includes worry, anxiety, and other unhealthy psychological involvement. The door of hatred includes bitterness, envy, and gossip.[24]

It is possible that these open doors were caused by past experiences, which are no longer a part of your present life. Perhaps you have not recognized past behavior as sinful, from which you needed to close the door—*"put off the old man"*—so that you can be set free. For example, perhaps you have visited a fortune teller who made you laugh as she told you your unlikely future. You thought it was a game. You did not realize that you opened a door in your mind for the occult to torment your soul. Paul clearly explained that when we yield ourselves to sin, we yield ourselves to bondage.

> *Know ye not, that to whom ye yield yourselves servants to obey, his servants ye are to whom ye obey; whether of sin unto death, or of obedience unto righteousness?* (Romans 6:16)

When you were born again, you may have received deliverance from sinful habits, freedom from hatred, and reconciliation in broken relationships. That is *sozo* salvation working in your soul. Yet the apostle Paul also taught in the New Testament that the Holy Spirit works in your soul *"until the day of Jesus Christ"*:

> *Being confident of this very thing, that he which hath begun a good work in you will perform it until the day of Jesus Christ....That ye may approve things that are excellent; that ye may be sincere and without offence till the day of Christ; being filled with the fruits of righteousness.* (Philippians 1:6, 10–11)

Paul exhorted believers to get rid of *"all bitterness, and wrath, and anger, and clamour, and evil speaking...with all malice* [or hatred]*"* (Ephesians 4:31). And he gave us a portrait of what a mentally and emotionally healthy believer should emulate: *"Be ye kind one to another,*

---

24. Please see Appendix for complete listing.

tenderhearted, forgiving one another, even as God for Christ's sake hath forgiven you" (Ephesians 4:32).

Paul explained that the work of the Holy Spirit in believers' lives is for the perfecting of the saints, *"till we all come in the unity of the faith, and of the knowledge of the Son of God, unto a perfect man, unto the measure of the stature of the fulness of Christ"* (Ephesians 4:13).

As a part of the sanctification process, we need to renounce any involvement in these areas of sin to be set free. Otherwise, we will settle for much less than *sozo* salvation. And learning to put off the old man and yield our souls to the redemptive work of the Holy Spirit involves the journey of a lifetime. In all of life's situations, we need to determine not to give place to the devil by holding on to offense, unforgiveness, or even the grief of unbearable loss. We need to recognize how the enemy gains access to our souls. Then we need to ask the Holy Spirit to shine His light in our souls to identify our bondage and close the doors of access, whether they are rooted in past or present wounds or sin.

> *In all of life's situations, we need to determine not to give place to the devil by holding on to offense, unforgiveness, or even the grief of unbearable loss.*

If you suffer from any of the emotional torments of fear, hatred, sexual sin, or occult involvement, or participate (or have participated) in any of the sinful acts associated with them (listed in the Appendix), you need to confess it to the Holy Spirit. As you repent, make sure to renounce the specific area of fear, hatred, etc., and ask for His cleansing by the blood of Jesus. He has promised to forgive and cleanse you from past, present, and future failing as you choose to walk in His light:

> *If we walk in the light, as he is in the light, we have fellowship one with another, and the blood of Jesus Christ his Son cleanseth us from all sin.... If we confess our sins, he is faithful and just to forgive us our sins, and to cleanse us from all unrighteousness.* (1 John 1:7, 9)

Jesus, the Bondage Breaker

Because we have not understood how to close these doors, thus ending Satan's advantage over our lives, many of us have been ruined by enemy's work to "kill, steal, and destroy." (See John 10:10.)

I know a woman named Julia who allowed the Holy Spirit to restore her life by breaking the grip of the enemy on her soul. Her story clearly shows how the enemy seduces us with the purpose of ruining our lives. It also shows us God's pathway to freedom and how He breaks the enemy's hold on our lives to establish us in wholeness.

Julia had no idea that the reckless lifestyle she was living was designed by Satan to keep her from the destiny God had planned for her. To her, it seemed harmless: she wanted to try the things that seemed to satisfy her curious nature. And at first, it was exciting to live on the dangerous edge of consequence, though her family often warned her: "Don't go to those kinds of places"; "Find a hardworking man and marry him"; "Be a faithful wife and raise children."

But Julia was confident that she could take care of herself. She didn't expect her parents to understand that she wanted to experience all the things they had missed out on. Her lifestyle seemed so glamorous. Maybe she would even become wealthy and famous. She just wanted a little space to live life on her terms.

Julia had an insatiable craving for personal attention, especially from men. She couldn't remember her father taking her on his lap and telling her that she was beautiful. He had not even spoken admiring words to her when she had been given the lead role in her school play. She remembered how it had hurt her to hear her friends' fathers telling them, "You are beautiful, my Princess." Her thought was, *What would that feel like? I wonder if I am beautiful. I want to be special to somebody.*

The first man who told her she was beautiful also told her that he loved her. And she couldn't bring herself to say no to his advances, though it was not her intention to be "that kind of woman." How could something that felt so good be so wrong? But within a few months of their involvement, she discovered that his words were simply a ploy to use her for his selfish pleasure.

That was the first of many times Julia was deceived into giving herself to a man—a poor trade to satisfy her craving for attention.

Eventually, life on her terms was living in a cheap hotel, using her beautiful personality, which God had given her to fulfill His calling on her life, to entice those who would pay her for her favors. One day, in order to cope with this lifestyle and muzzle the cries of her conscience, which was foreign to her upbringing, she tried a line of cocaine. When that became a daily habit, it dawned on Julia what a terrible habit had formed to give her a few hours of relief.

Who would have dreamed that the innocent girl who carried her little white Bible to church on Sundays and helped Grandma make fried apple pies would find herself in such a miserable, wasted state? We dare not underestimate Satan's power to deceive us into thinking that the sure road to stardom we have chosen is actually a treacherous path to destruction.

Julia's days and nights began to run together. Her life became a blur; her main goal was trying to get a little more money to buy a few more drugs. People became players, mere passing objects. Life had used her and tossed her aside. No one heard her cries for help.

Then one day, she remembered the Jesus she had read about in her little white Bible. She looked at an old, familiar picture of Him sitting by a well, talking to a woman no one else would talk to. Like Julia, this woman had gone from man to man, unable to find satisfaction, even with five husbands. The Holy Spirit softened Julia's heart and reminded her of the pure and compassionate love she had seen in Jesus' eyes in that picture. In her misery, she wondered, *If He would talk to her, would He talk to me?*

That divinely breathed thought was the beginning of Julia's breakthrough. She asked Jesus to forgive her for turning from Him, and once she felt His loving embrace, she became like the woman in the Scriptures who poured out the contents of her alabaster box on Jesus, worshipping at His feet. She could not believe that He would let her experience His pure love so deeply within her aching soul.

She just continued to pour out all she had before Him in worship, because, for the first time in her life, she understood that her life was of great value to Him. Later, she read what Jesus said about the sinful woman who worshiped at His feet: "Who is forgiven much loves much." (See Luke 7:47.) Then she understood why she was filled with such deep love for her Master.

For many years, Julia has walked with the Lord. She is now free and on track with her destiny, which she almost missed. She shared with me that she had come to understand that the problem that thrust her life forward to destruction was not the sin of fornication; that was merely a symptom. It stemmed from the deep wound in her psyche caused by her father's lack of affirmation. Through the ministry she had received, she had come to grips with the root of her problem, and what it had caused.

Without the security of her father's love, she lacked a sense of identity and self-worth. So she began to look for affirmation in all the wrong places. Once the Holy Spirit opened her eyes to this, Julia was so relieved and thankful to God that He had made a provision to salvage her thrown-away life—not just to rescue her to take her to heaven but also to reveal Himself to her in such a way that she was being made whole in His presence.

The Holy Spirit taught her that it was her responsibility to close the doors she had opened to the enemy in her life. She renounced the sins of rebellion, fornication, and drug addiction; she renounced her promiscuous lifestyle; and she renounced the lie that she must find someone to affirm her as a woman. In making these choices, the Holy Spirit empowered her to close the door to a lifestyle that had been destroying her.

Then, Julia prayed for God to break the soul ties she had with all those with whom she had been wrongly involved. Finally, she began to forgive those whom she perceived were part of her demise. That forgiveness became the last key to breaking her chains. She forgave her father for not being the dad she needed him to be. She forgave the first man who deceived her and seduced her. And she forgave her "friends of the trade," who enticed her into participating in their lifestyle. One by one, she forgave her offenders; and tearfully, she yielded every trace of bitterness and desire for revenge.

When she finished telling me her story, her eyes were moist. She said to me, "This is why I love Jesus so much. He loved me out of my sin and out of my bondage. And when I understood I had to forgive those whom I blamed for leading me astray, He helped me to make that hard choice. I never dreamed that by forgiving those who had hurt me, I would be set free, no longer a victim of the damage they perpetrated in my life."

The Keys to Healing

Julia understands the powerful truth of Jesus' words, *"If the Son therefore shall make you free, ye shall be free indeed"* (John 8:36). She learned to use the keys of renouncing sin and forgiving her enemies to receive the divine healing she needed in her psyche. A closer look at these two biblical keys may help you to receive healing and freedom, as well.

Renouncing Sin

> [We] *have renounced the hidden things of dishonesty, not walking in craftiness, nor handling the word of God deceitfully; but by manifestation of the truth commending ourselves to every man's conscience in the sight of God.*   (2 Corinthians 4:2)

The apostle Paul declared that, as believers, we have *"renounced"* the hidden things of dishonesty and craftiness; and we do not handle the Word of God deceitfully. To renounce something means to forbid it or to give it up.[25] There is a difference between feeling sorry for something—even asking forgiveness for something—and renouncing all involvement in that thing.

When we renounce *"hidden things,"* we are separating ourselves completely from them. We forbid their work in our lives from that moment on. For example, a person may be willing to ask for forgiveness for committing adultery. He may feel sorry for his sin and yet not be persuaded in his mind that the adulterous relationship itself is wrong. But when he *renounces* adultery, his mind-set is reversed. He forbids it and gives up any thought of tolerating it ever again.

> *When we renounce hidden things, we are separating ourselves completely from them. We forbid their work in our lives from that moment on.*

For Julia, the miracle of renouncing sin and turning from it became a reality. She started to hate the very thing that once appeared glamorous and intriguing to her. She no longer considered her destructive lifestyle desirable or acceptable. She renounced them from her life—this is true freedom.

25. *Strong's,* #G550.

I have found that, beyond asking for forgiveness of a particular sin, it is absolutely liberating to renounce it. It puts me totally on the side of God, who hates sin. And it has the power to close the door to the enemy's temptation. There has been no crack left open where he can wedge his way back into my life. And I believe it is important to renounce *"the hidden things"* audibly before God. The Scriptures from both the Old and New Testament give credence to the power of life and death that is in the tongue. (See Proverbs 18:21.)

Forgiving Others

Jesus understands how deeply we have been hurt. He understands the pain caused by the insensitive, uncaring acts and words of others. And He arranged for our redemption by sending His Son, Jesus Christ, to shed His blood at Calvary. There is no other way to be set free from the painful consequences of sin—your sins and the ways in which others have sinned against you—apart from accepting Christ's sacrifice for sin.

We have discussed the responsibility we have to forgive others, especially when we have received God's forgiveness for such a great debt of sin when we were born again. When we choose to forgive those who have sinned against us, we may be surprised at the liberating release it brings to our own souls.

You can forgive others regardless of their desire or ability to ever make things right with you. Even if they hate you, they cannot keep you from experiencing the freedom that comes when you forgive them. Forgiveness releases you from holding on to the hatred and resentment you feel toward your enemy. It opens the door to your prison of emotional bondage, which was built by those negative attitudes.

I stated earlier that forgiveness is the one gift we have been given that can set us free, making us victors instead of victims. It is simply a fact that many times, people are not even aware of the emotional pain they have caused us. But, whether perceived or real, we must choose to forgive their offense if we are to walk in the wholeness Christ died to give us.

Forgiveness is the one gift we have been given that can set us free, making us victors instead of victims.

HEALING FOR YOUR LOSSES

Throughout these pages, I have shared with you the revelation of freedom for my soul that God was so faithful to bring to me by His Holy Spirit. He has allowed me to drink more deeply from that cup of *sozo* freedom, which Jesus provided for us. During my years of ministry, I have tasted this divine freedom and experienced wholeness in areas of my soul. I have enjoyed His peace and joy in serving Him. And I believe that from the moment we are born again, our journey toward wholeness begins, and then it continues throughout life.

But the recent liberating work God has done in my soul has greatly deepened my love for Him. It has opened my prison doors and launched me into realms of freedom I had never imagined possible. As a result, my heart has been filled with a deeper compassion for others who suffer from hidden wounds, of which they may not be aware.

I fully expect the Holy Spirit to continue His sanctifying work in my soul, and I am sure He will shine His light on other low-swimming fish that hinder me from the wholeness He wants me to experience. I have not arrived at perfection, but because of my recent encounter with God, I have embraced this journey toward *sozo*—complete wholeness—with a new perspective on freedom. As I have shared, the Lord has shined His light on the unhealed areas of my soul during the months of my pain and suffering. And as I yielded to His cleansing work, He set me free. I now have greater understanding of the psalmist's declaration, *"He restoreth my soul"* (Psalm 23:3). It is in that greater light that I continually ask Him to show me areas of my soul that need to be healed. And I am determined to continually surrender my soul to His cleansing work.

Of course, life still presents difficult and painful challenges that must be handled correctly. When people or situations hurt us, we must choose to forgive and to renounce sin, as needed. Then we will find that this deeper experience of healing has taken the fear out of facing future challenges. And the more whole we are, the more we are established in God's love. He will enlarge our capacity to show His healing love to others.

Because of His healing work in my soul, I do not fear that others' hurtful actions or attitudes toward me will find a home in my wounded psyche, because the wounds no longer exists. The lies have been canceled, and God's healing truth prevails. In their place, God's compassion abides, and it can flow through me to discern the wounds of others and pray for the restoration of their soul.

Becoming a First Partaker of the Fruits

My first mentor taught me a biblical principle that has become a guiding light in my life. On one occasion, when I was bemoaning a difficult time of pressure and trial that I was experiencing, she said to me, "Always remember, honey, *'the husbandman that laboureth must be first partaker of the fruits'* (2 Timothy 2:6)." There is a natural logic in the statement that a farmer is entitled to his own crop. However, I understood her spiritual interpretation to mean that I must walk in forgiveness if I want to effectively minister the truth of forgiveness to others as a teacher and mentor.

At that time, I was new to my walk with God. So, I reasoned, *she's probably wrong. I think I can avoid a lot of the suffering others have gone through if I can learn to stay ahead of the game.* I didn't like the prospect of having to suffer difficult experiences to learn the ways of God. I thought that I could find an easier way than the one that my mentor was describing.

But, I soon learned that there is no way to avoid *life*. We cannot predict the unexpected. Our interactions with difficult people and situations can't always be controlled; and they *are* unpredictable. For example, as a pastor, there is no way I can predict the negative actions or attitudes of some people to insulate myself from future disappointments; it goes with the territory. Neither is it possible for anyone to avoid unwanted sickness or attacks of the enemy. If we think we can somehow harden our hearts to escape inevitable disappointments in life, we sabotage our own capacity to be tenderhearted ministers of Jesus' love to others. Tenderhearted people will get hurt.

> *There is no way to avoid life. We cannot predict the unexpected.*

Avoiding pain is not the answer to living victoriously as a Christian or fulfilling our divine destiny. The answer is to appropriate Christ's provision of *sozo*, to give Him continual access to our souls. He will heal our broken hearts and lead us into wholeness.

My mentor understood what it means to be empowered to help others; it comes from walking in victory in our own souls. Compassion for others is released in our lives when we surrender to God's healing power amidst suffering. Only then can we truly say to others in their distress, "I feel your pain." The apostle Paul taught this powerful principle of comforting others as we are comforted in our trials:

> *Blessed be God, even the Father of our Lord Jesus Christ, the Father of mercies, and the God of all comfort; who comforteth us in all our tribulation, that we may be able to comfort them which are in any trouble, by the comfort wherewith we ourselves are comforted of God.*
> (2 Corinthians 1:3–4)

No Loss Is Too Great

In previous chapters, we have discussed several causes of painful loss that wound our minds. First, we must deal with our personal sin. We must recognize that we are born into sin and iniquity simply because we are a fallen human race.

(See Psalm 51:5.) Until we receive Christ as our Savior, there is no hope of living in freedom and wholeness, with a sound mind and healthy emotions.

We also suffer from the sins or "unlove" committed against our souls by other imperfect people. Whether from friends or siblings, parents or other authority figures, real or perceived wounds caused by others will affect us our entire lives, from our birth to death. Even Christian families are vulnerable to sin and offense on their journeys to becoming more Christlike.

The terrible grief of losing a loved one, whether to death, divorce, or other cause of estrangement, deeply wounds our minds. Books have been written to help us through various stages of grief so that we can move forward with our lives. My mother shared her grief with me when she lost her husband to divorce. She felt that the pain of divorce was greater than it would have been to lose him to death because of the deep rejection she felt, which is often a by-product of divorce. Both death and divorce cause deep wounds in our souls, and we need healing for both.

Losing a relative you dearly love is deeply painful. It is life altering. Losing a friendship through a misunderstanding or betrayal also wounds our psyches. Losing a position in service or employment that is part of your identity causes a deep sense of loss, as well. Even the loss of personal health can cause unbearable grief. Often, depression accompanies such losses and can become so debilitating that we are unable to function. Our lives become meaningless when we lose relationships or the pride we had in a career.

The list of losses that wound us is long, and deeply personal. Whether perceived or real, the pain of loss is the same. In short, when Jesus fulfilled the prophecy of coming to earth to *"healeth the broken in heart, and bindeth up their wounds"* (Psalm 147:3), He must have known that not one person was exempt from this need of divine healing and restoration of the soul.

Even as Christians, we haven't realized how much Jesus wants to heal us from our losses.

I believe that one of the biggest reasons why we can't seem to set to the other side of bad things that happen to us is that, even as Christians, we haven't realized how much Jesus wants to heal us from our losses. When we have lost relationships, positions, or possessions, and see no way for them to be recovered, painful grief is a natural reaction. We would not be normal if we did not suffer deeply in the face of loss. But if we expect to live a victorious life in Christ, we must not adopt the victim mind-set. It is because life happens that we desperately need a divine Healer to restore our souls.

> *We must not adopt the victim mind-set if we expect to live a victorious life in Christ.*

Restoring the Loss from Our Personal Sin

Earlier, we discussed the moral failure of King David, even though the Scriptures describe him as *"a man after [God's] own heart"* (1 Samuel 13:14). He was God's chosen king of Israel, and he was a devout worshiper of God, restoring the Ark of the Covenant—the presence of God—to Israel.

We could say that King David was really messed up. Yet he shows us the way to restoration from the loss of personal sin. He cried out to God, *"Restore unto me the joy of thy salvation; and uphold me with thy free spirit"* (Psalm 51:12). David confessed his sin, begging God to forgive and cleanse him and to create a clean heart in him.

What depth of compassion and forgiveness fills the heart of God for fallen mankind! Only as we seek His divine intervention to heal our soul from its inborn iniquity (see Psalm 51:5) can we be healed from our losses caused by sin. For lack of this repentance some believers do not walk in freedom. They have no confidence to minister to others what they have not received for themselves. David understood that until he was cleansed and was restored the *"joy of [God's] salvation,"* he could not minister to others:

> *Then will I teach transgressors thy ways; and sinners shall be converted unto thee.* (Psalm 51:13)

Restoring the Loss When Sinned Against

We discussed briefly the terrible pain that Joseph suffered when his jealous brothers sinned against him. Sold into slavery, he was separated from his family and country for many years. Still, he lived by the godly principles he had been taught. From the status of a slave, he rose to power in a notable household in Egypt, only to be set up once again by his master's wife, who tried to seduce him.

Thrown into prison by his master, he still maintained his relationship with God and was put in charge of the prison. Over and over, the Scriptures affirm that the favor of God was with Joseph. (See Genesis 39:21.) In prison, he used his favor to interpret the dream of Pharaoh, which eventually lifted him out of his misery and into his destiny. Pharaoh made him the second most powerful ruler in Egypt.

If Joseph had allowed hatred and bitterness to seethe in his soul, how different the outcome of his life would have been. While his suffering and loss was real, he allowed God to keep him during those painful years. The Scriptures confirm that *"until the time that his word came: the word of the LORD tried him"* (Psalm 105:19).

During his years of suffering, he discovered his destiny and became the "savior" of Israel, even rescuing his family from great famine. His forgiving attitude toward those who sinned against him should inspire us. He said to his brothers, *"It was not you that sent me hither, but God…But as for you, ye thought evil against me; but God meant it unto good, to bring to pass, as it is this day, to save much people alive"* (Genesis 45:8, 50:20). Joseph's life is an example of the divine restoration the apostle Paul spoke of when talking of all kinds of suffering:

> *And we know that all things work together for good to them that love God, to them who are the called according to his purpose.*
>
> (Romans 8:28)

Loss is real. It is painful. In a sense, many painful losses are unrecoverable—the loss of a loved one, loss of relationships, financial loss. But the promise of God is that if we choose to love Him and allow His love to permeate our lives, He will work together even the most painful events in our lives—*all* things—for our good. Paul wrote a formidable list of *"all things"* and declared that not one of them could destroy our soul:

> *Nay, in all these things we are more than conquerors through him that loved us. For I am persuaded, that neither death, nor life, nor angels, nor*

principalities, nor powers, nor things present, nor things to come, nor height, nor depth, nor any other creature, shall be able to separate us from the love of God, which is in Christ Jesus our Lord. (Romans 8:37–39)

> *If we love God and allow His love to permeate our lives, He will work together even the most painful events in our lives—all things—for our good.*

We have confined our discussion of pain and loss primarily to the causes reiterated above. Whether life's losses come to us willfully, unintentionally, or through our own wrong choices, the end result is the same: the pain of an unhealed mind. Life seems much more hopeless when we think it is up to us to solve all our problems, to resolve our pain. When we try to rearrange our lives after painful changes have been forced upon us, we may have difficulty not blaming others and focusing on our pain. But when we trust the God that loves us, we allow Him to turn all things for our good.

The iniquity into which we are all born results in the human condition Jesus described as "brokenhearted, bruised, and captive." We must understand and trust that He came to heal our hearts and to save our souls—completely. The writer to the Hebrews gave us this wonderful promise:

*Wherefore [Jesus] is able also to save them to the **uttermost** that come unto God by him, seeing he ever liveth to make intercession for them.*
(Hebrews 7:25)

As seen in the stories I have shared of people who have experienced *sozo*, complete healing can become a reality for every believer. We simply need to yield to the cleansing work of the Holy Spirit as He shines His light into our wounded soul.

The Loss That All Disciples Experience

As we conclude our study, I want to mention one other inevitable source of loss that Jesus said all His followers would encounter. He explained to His disciples that there is a cost of discipleship for all who choose to follow Him:

If any man will come after me, let him deny himself, and take up his cross, and follow me. For whosoever will save his life shall lose it: and whosoever will lose his life for my sake shall find it. (Matthew 16:24–25)

The disciples had left everything behind to follow Christ. On one occasion, Peter asked the Lord, "*Behold, we have forsaken all, and followed thee; what shall we have therefore?*" (Matthew 19:27). First, Jesus promised that they would sit upon twelve thrones, judging the twelve tribes of Israel. (See Matthew 19:28.) Then, He extended the following promise to all who follow Him:

And every one that hath forsaken houses, or brethren, or sisters, or father, or mother, or wife, or children, or lands, for my name's sake, shall receive an hundredfold, and shall inherit everlasting life. (Matthew 19:29)

It was a happy day for me when I discovered that God had a plan to restore my losses—the costs of my discipleship—a "*hundredfold.*" I read Jesus' promise over and over again and allowed His amazing words to sink deeply into my heart. Yet it still seemed too good to be true. But I reasoned, *It is Jesus Himself making this promise to every believer. I know that I can fully believe it.*

What comfort and joy fills our hearts when we embrace God's promise to give "*an hundredfold*" to all who know the cost involved in becoming His disciple. As we follow Him to work in our lives, and as we renounce our sin and forgive others, He heals our soul from every painful loss. And He opens His loving heart to give us gifts that far exceed the losses we have suffered.

I have found that what God gives in return for surrendering to His purposes is not just something little to replace what I had lost. He gives me *more* of what I lost, as He blessed me in my relationships and finances. In fact, I have learned that during seasons of relational or financial loss, there opens a doorway to increase! Perhaps that is the significance, at least in part of Jesus' admonition in His call to discipleship:

He that loveth father or mother more than me is not worthy of me: and he that loveth son or daughter more than me is not worthy of me. And he that taketh not his cross, and followeth after me, is not worthy of me. He

that findeth his life shall lose it: and he that loseth his life for my sake shall
find it. (Matthew 10:37–39)

The willingness to lose our lives for His sake, to surrender our minds, emotions, and wills—our souls—to His divine will for our lives, can involve painful losses. But Jesus has promised that we will truly find our lives when we surrender continually to the destiny He has ordained for each of us. Not only will He heal our brokenness, but He also will restore us to pursue His God-given purposes for our lives, which alone can satisfy our souls. Only God in His infinite goodness can devise such a plan.

A Greater Capacity to Love

I also learned that, no matter how great my loss was, as I chose to forgive who needed to be forgiven, to repent what needed to be repented of, and to humbly surrender to God, God worked my suffering for my good. In addition, He blessed the work of my hands with favor, and He opened doors for me to touch more hurting people with the wonderful truths of the gospel. God created in me a greater capacity for His love than I had experienced ever before. And God filled that larger space with greater compassion for hurting people.

I was able to trust God in a greater way than I had before He rescued my soul from those painful situations. I understood that if God could bring me through my "hopeless" situation into victory, I could trust Him for greater deliverance than what I had trusted Him for before. In short, He was working all things together for my good. (See Romans 8:28.)

As I recovered from my serious illness and rejoiced in the inner healing He had done in my soul, I felt like the Holy Spirit said to me, "The time for grieving is over. Lift up your eyes and watch for the hundredfold restoration I am sending to you." I had a greater expectancy to receive His promise. And watching for the fulfillment of that promise was the way I could express my faith. I became more than encouraged. I was excited. What was my life going to look like when I received what He had for me?

So it was that as I watched, God worked. He changed situations in my life and ministry. He opened new doors for fruitfulness. And He brought new people into my life who, in turn, connected me with other new people. In short, He set my feet on the pathway to greater blessing. It is simply a fact that God will never be any man's debtor. If we give freely and sacrificially to Him (or for Him), He has promised a great payback. And He follows through with His promise.

> *If we give freely and sacrificially to God (or for God), He has promised a great payback.*

Letting Go of What You Lost

Of course, all of this restoration requires change—both in us and in our life situations. It is not always easy to embrace change, even if we know they are better for us and will enlarge our capacity for good things. We are comfortable with the familiar. This is why we desperately need Jesus to restore our souls, so that we are no longer willing to settle for less than what He desires for us.

We must continually embrace the reality of our need for sanctification—for wholeness. Our souls remain weak and sickly if we do not yield to this work of the Holy Spirit. In fact, we will likely stay stymied in our desire to serve God unless we open our hearts to His light. Accepting the truth of our sinful, wounded condition is requisite to receiving His healing and restoration.

To repent of our own sin is to let go of our false righteousness and receive the righteousness of God, as He cleanses us of our sin. To forgive another person of their sin is to let go of that injustice, in opposition to what we felt like we deserved. To accept the painful losses of life, we must let go of our love for that which we lost. I heard Pastor T. D. Jakes say, "You can only rebuild on what you have left, not what you have lost."

> *We have to rebuild on what we have instead of continually yearning for what we have lost.*

This seems obvious, but the human psyche has a hard time letting go of what it loved or preferred, especially when we suffer life-altering changes like the loss of close relationships. We have to tell ourselves to get over it. In order to receive the restoration God promises, we must push through our own pain and receive His health in our souls, His favor in our life situations. When we do that, His grace and His Spirit are then free to sustain us and finish their sanctifying work in our lives.

The Old Testament patriarch Job was considered to be a perfect man by God Himself. Yet the losses he endured were overwhelming; they included all those things Jesus mentions. (See Matthew 10:37–39.) Job lost his children, his property, and in a sense, his wife, who taunted him in his misery. He even lost his physical health. His closest "friends" made life more miserable for him. His life seemed over; he was reduced to a trash heap, left with no explanation to his deplorable condition.

Yet God showed Job (as He does with us) His desire to recompense those who submit to Him, no matter what. He rewarded Job's trusting heart with twice as much as she'd had before:

> And the Lord turned the captivity of Job, when he prayed for his friends: also the Lord gave Job twice as much as he had before....So the Lord blessed the latter end of Job more than his beginning.   (Job 42:10, 12)

Trials and difficulties, seeming setbacks or failures, even great losses in our lives don't need to keep us from God's blessing and favor or from fulfilling His destiny for our lives. We need only to understand and embrace God's promise to heal and restore our souls, to rescue us from the plan of the enemy, and to give to us His abundant life. He is a Rescuer. He is the Restorer of our souls. This is His will and His promise to us.

Let me encourage your heart to trust God for His complete salvation in your soul. Don't settle for anything less than what His *sozo* salvation provides...

+ Wholeness, sanctification, peace, and joy in the Holy Spirit;

+ The fellowship of the Father, the Son, and the Holy Spirit in this life, not just in eternity;

✦ And fulfillment of our destiny, which will satisfy the deepest yearning in your soul for significance.

No matter how impossible you think your situation is, how great your losses, how irretrievable the past blessings you've enjoyed, consider one of God's many promises to restore your fortunes:

And I will restore to you the years that the locust hath eaten, the canker-worm, and the caterpillar, and the palmerworm, my great army which I sent among you. (Joel 2:25)

Each of these worms destroys a different part of a healthy tree, such as the leaves and the bark. So this analogy of God's powerful work of redemption tells us that He is able to restore each part of us that has been ravaged by enemy hoards. God not only restores the fortunes of righteous men like Job. He also offers His total restoration to those who have sabotaged their own lives. He redeems those who have blown it, just as He did for the prodigal son. After Isaiah prophesied the purpose of the Lord to heal the broken-hearted, he continued drawing his beautiful portrait of our Savior:

Because the LORD *hath anointed me…to appoint unto them that mourn in Zion, to give unto them beauty for ashes, the oil of joy for mourning, the garment of praise for the spirit of heaviness; that they might be called trees of righteousness, the planting of the* LORD, *that he might be glorified.* (Isaiah 61:1, 3)

God restores us, that we might be *"trees of righteousness."* How different this is from shattered lives that are devastated by locusts and other destructive worms. The promises of God to make beauty for ashes and joy for mourning are applicable to every born-again believer. The Father wants to clothe you with the *"robe of righteousness"* (Isaiah 61:10) of His Son; He wants to give you the "garment of praise" by His Spirit; and He wants to reveal His righteousness to you, that He might be glorified.

Because of God's wonderful promises to those who surrender their lives to Him, there is life after loss and a future after failure. Out of the ashes of burned up dreams and burned out efforts, God promises His beauty.

There is life after loss and a future after failure.
Out of the ashes of burned up dreams and burned out efforts,
God promises His beauty.

There simply is no unredeemable situation that you can present to God. The key is to present *yourself* to Him and to humbly submit to His sanctifying work in your soul. You will find life and reap great reward, and you will be equipped to share His redeeming love and power with others—this is the essence of spiritual breakthrough.

APPENDIX: THE FOUR DOORS[26]

By Argentinian Pastor Pablo Bottari

Fear:

- Worry
- Unbelief
- Need to control
- Anxiety
- Isolation
- Apathy
- Drugs/alcohol

Sexual sin:

- Adultery
- Pornography
- Fornication
- Lewdness
- Molestation

---

26. Dawna De Silva and Teresa Liebscher, *Sozo Basic Training Manual*, 38.

+ Rape

Hatred:

+ Bitterness
+ Envy
+ Gossiping
+ Slander
+ Anger
+ Self-hatred or low self-worth

Occult/Witchcraft:

+ Astrology
+ Fortune Telling
+ Reading Tarot Cards
+ Séances
+ Ouija boards
+ Manipulation
+ Participation in Covens
+ Casting Curses/Witchcraft practices

ABOUT THE AUTHOR

In 1973, Sue Curran and her husband, John, founded Shekinah Church in Blountville, Tennessee. For years, Pastor Curran has been teaching on the importance of prayer in the church, a topic that is very close to her heart. In doing so, she is fulfilling her spiritual calling to create a "house of prayer" in both individuals and the body of Christ.

Pastor Curran is a much sought-after speaker at leadership conferences and prayer conferences, both in the US and abroad. She has also hosted many of her own. Her wit and prophetic wisdom make her a powerful teacher and minister. Her real-life experiences draw people in, and her teachings on how to create a dynamic prayer life have attracted a large group of supporters, including many ministry leaders and mentors.

Curran is now an adjunct professor at Christian Life School of Theology Global in Columbus, Georgia, where she received her master's degree in theology, as well as her Doctorate of Divinity. She continues spreading the message on the importance of prayer and desires to see that message transform the lives of all believers.